The Rules for Online Dating

Capturing the Heart of Mr. Right in Cyberspace

ELLEN FEIN *and* SHERRIE SCHNEIDER

POCKET BOOKS
New York London Toronto Sydney Singapore

An *Original* Publication of POCKET BOOKS

 POCKET BOOKS, a division of Simon & Schuster, Inc.
1230 Avenue of the Americas, New York, NY 10020

Copyright © 2002 by Ellen Fein and Sherrie Schneider

ISBN: 0-7434-5147-3

First Pocket Books trade paperback printing July 2002

10 9 8 7 6 5 4 3 2 1

POCKET and colophon are registered trademarks of Simon & Schuster, Inc.

For information regarding special discounts for bulk purchases, please contact Simon & Schuster Special Sales at 1-800-456-6798 or business@simonandschuster.com

Book design by Helene Berinsky
Cover design by Pink Elephant

Printed in the U.S.A.

CONTENTS

ACKNOWLEDGMENTS

We would like to thank our families and friends; our agents at Clausen, Mays & Tahan literary agency, Stedman Mays and especially Mary Tahan, who believed in and supported us in writing this book; and our editor at Pocket Books/Simon & Schuster, Mitchell Ivers, who made it all possible. And thanks to all the *Rules* girls online around the world who e-mailed us their experiences, tips, and success stories!

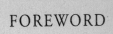

Meet the First Online *Rules* Girl

Staci was 29 years old, very pretty with big blue eyes, and she was tired of the dating scene. When her last relationship ended, she bought a computer.

While her friends were still club-hopping to meet guys and online dating was still in its infancy, Staci put up an ad with her photo. There was no support back then for Staci to be doing this, but she read *The Rules* and applied the principles of real-life dating to cyberspace dating the best she could and told all her friends what she was doing.

Being a *Rules* girl, she made up a catchy screen name, StaciBlueEyez29. She kept her ad light and breezy—nothing about finding her soul mate or how her last relationship ended badly—and tried to answer the questionnaires as briefly as possible.

It never occurred to Staci to answer a man's ad since that would be like approaching a man at a bar and talking to him first. She just knew it was best if men pursued her. She received more than 200 responses in three months. She screened heavily, eliminating married men; men who sent "winks" (an impersonal way to respond to an ad by the mere push of a key), smiles, photos with no words, and form letters; and men who had racy screen names.

She waited 24 to 48 hours to respond to e-mails so that she appeared busy and mysterious, although deep down inside she was anxious to meet a nice guy.

She discarded the impulse to respond right away, so that she wouldn't appear too eager.

She did all this in spite of her fear that not responding sooner would make some men move on to other women.

Staci also filled up her weekends with dates and other activities so that she wasn't on the computer on Saturday nights looking like Ms. Lonely Hearts Club. When occasionally she was home and on the computer on a Friday or Saturday night, she blocked herself so that no one would know she was online and forced herself not to answer any e-mails from men. She knew nothing could be less *Rules*-y than a guy you don't know finding out you have nothing better to do on a Saturday night than sit at home and answer his e-mail.

In her responses to men who e-mailed her, Staci kept her e-mails short—only two or three sentences. She always waited until men specifically asked for her telephone number, and then gave them her cell phone number only. She never revealed where she lived or worked and agreed to meet in a public place for a quick drink for "date zero." (Date zero is the first time a woman meets a man she's never met before but has been corresponding with online through a dating website or a chat room.) She always told her mother or a friend the men's e-mail addresses, telephone numbers, any other pertinent info she had about them, and where she was going and when. She would spend an hour or two with her dates and act upbeat, even if they weren't "the right one." And she always ended the dates first.

After several months of disappointing dates with men who were not as nice as their e-mails, or not as good-looking as their photos, she wanted to take her ad down. Instead, she formed a formal support group of online *Rules* friends to keep her going. Staci found herself e-mailing her *Rules* support friends one horror story after another until GuyForYou245 answered her ad.

After GuyForYou245—Brad—asked her to be exclusive, Staci took down her ad. He proposed nine months later.

Staci is not ashamed to tell people she met her fiancé this way. She still tells friends and acquaintances who are not meeting men and don't care for bars and clubs, "Put on your sweatpants, sweep up your hair in a clip, pick out your best picture, put up an ad, and follow *The Rules*. It really works!"

Who's the Father?!

A young woman sat in the doctor's office receiving the news of her pregnancy. She didn't look too happy, and when the doctor inquired, she explained that there had been several men in the past few months.

"I won't know who the father is!"

"Well, you may want to contact each of them and have them come in for DNA testing. Then you'll know for sure," said the doctor.

"I can't do that," the young lady replied.

"Why not?" asked the doctor.

"Because they've all changed their screen names!"

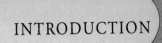

What *The Rules* Are and Why They Work

For those of you who are not familiar with *The Rules: Time-Tested Secrets for Capturing the Heart of Mr. Right,* our best-selling dating book published in 1995, it was the first book to come clean about what men really want from women they date. The fact is, men love a challenge; therefore women need to play hard to get. In essence, *The Rules* is a set of behaviors guaranteed to help a man fall in love with a woman *after* he shows initial interest. But *he* must show the initial interest—not you.

Specifically, we told women:

- Don't talk to a man first; otherwise, how will you know if he was truly smitten enough by you to strike up a conversation with you first?
- Don't call him. Calling a man puts you in the position of pursuer. Men love a chase.
- Don't accept a Saturday night date after Wednesday. If he can call you at the last minute and get to see you, he

won't think you are so special. And you'll be setting a bad precedent for the whole relationship. He has to put effort in to see you.

- No more than casual kissing, if even that, on the first date. Sleeping with men too soon is the kiss of death for a long-term relationship. The longer it takes for the physical side of the relationship to catch up to the emotional side, the better.

- Don't open up too fast. Dating isn't therapy. Make him wait to find out all about you.

- Don't live with a man unless you're engaged with a wedding date; otherwise what incentive will he have to marry you?

- Don't date a married man. That's a dead end, for sure.

And we included more than 25 other *Rules* to help women catch Mr. Right.

In 1994, when we set out to write our first book, there was a plethora of dating books that we found to be completely unhelpful. They told women to do whatever they feel like, such as ask men out, go Dutch treat on a date, have sex on the first date, take men to couples counseling, and make men open up about their feelings. They claimed that it was the nineties and that women—especially powerful, professional women such as doctors, lawyers, [MBAs], Wall Street traders, and so on—no longer had to wait for men to make the first move. After all, these books said women were working the same jobs and commanding the same salaries as men. Why couldn't they act like men on dates?

Wow, did we wish this was true. Wow, did we wish we could just go to a party and talk to the really cute guy on the other side of the room, even if he didn't approach us. We could wish all we want, but the reality was something else. What the other dating books didn't get is this: *Work and dating are not the same.* A woman can go to Harvard Law School just like a man and make the same salary at a law firm and even clobber that man in court, but let her try to apply that aggression to dating and she's bound to lose out. Time and again, she'll hear that the guy wasn't interested, or that he "wanted space," or that he dumped her for the *other* girl—the one *he* spoke to first, the one who allowed mystery and romance to happen.

Making the first move on a man just doesn't work. Of course it doesn't, because work is intellectual, while dating is emotional. You can't make a man fall in love with you by asking him out and paying for his lunch. He has to feel a spark, seek you out, and at some level jump through hoops to *get* you to go out with him; that's the only way he'll commit to you and hopefully marry you.

Women complain that men won't commit. But we say, "Oh, yes, men *will* commit"—if they speak to you first and then you let them pursue you by playing hard to get. Men will avoid you if you pursue them. Equal legal rights and equal pay for women in the workplace cannot change a man's basic romantic nature. So our feeling is *vive la différence!* Stop trying to be equal with men in dating, just do what works.

Don't take our word for it. Do *The Rules* on a man and see what happens, and then don't do *The Rules* on a man and see what happens. The answer will be as obvious to you as it was to us and countless other women around the world. It may take time for you to fully accept the reality of *The Rules;* everybody gets it when they are ready. Unfortunately, that is usually after a painful non-*Rules* relationship fails.

Our first book struck a chord the first year it came out,

despite the fact that some women just didn't want to believe they couldn't call men or make things happen—especially if these women had big salaries and owned their own homes and were powerful in other areas of their lives. Some complained that we were old-fashioned and not feminists. We countered that if something works, it doesn't matter how old the recipe is, just do it. We maintain that we are, indeed, feminists: We are both ambitious and powerful women. We have written a best-selling book that was translated into 27 languages. We've formed our own company and we offer seminars, worldwide contacts and support groups, a newsletter *(The Rules News),* and private phone and e-mail consultations. And we did all that without a man. If that isn't feminism, what is?

Two million women worldwide agreed with us enough to buy our book. They were sick and tired of well-meaning strategies that didn't work in real life. Even therapists agreed that women needed to set boundaries, that do-what-you-feel-like dating doesn't work, so much so that we revised our chapter "Don't Discuss *The Rules* with your Therapist" in our first book to "You Can Ask Your Therapist to Help You Do *The Rules*" in our second book, *The Rules II: More Rules to Live and Love By. The Rules* became not just a *New York Times* best-seller but a worldwide phenomenon. We were mentioned in countless magazine stories and TV shows. We were on *Oprah* twice. We hit a nerve. Women were accepting that—like it or not—*The Rules* worked.

Our mailbox was jammed with letters, many success stories of engagements and wedding invitations, and also requests for advice. Thus was born our second and third books, *The Rules II,* for special situations such as long-distance dating, office romances, and dating a man who is separated, and *The Rules for Marriage.*

Now you are reading our online dating book. Why? Obviously, you are using the Internet to meet men or you've met a man in person and are communicating via e-mail a lot but you are not sure exactly how to do it. You don't want to blow it and you know you can without concrete guidelines. Worry no more!

We interviewed hundreds of women on the Internet over the last two years to find out what works and what doesn't. The good news is that *The Rules* do apply to online dating, so you don't have to make needless mistakes or waste time in your search for Mr. Right. So read on, and good luck in cyberspace!

E-mail and *The Rules* for Online Dating

E-mail has become a universal part of relationships these days, whether a relationship starts online or not. Millions of women around the world are "e-dating," whether they meet men online or in a local bar. In the last two years, we've seen a rapid shift in our consulting business—today about 50 to 75 percent of the calls and e-mails we get concern relationships being conducted on the Internet. And these women have been asking us for a book of *Rules* for dating online.

As many of you know, our first book, *The Rules,* spawned a worldwide movement. Readers began—and continue—to set up free online and offline support groups around the world and visit our website (www.therulesbook.com) at the rate of over 400,000 hits a month. But when we wrote *The Rules* seven years ago, little was known about online dating—many even considered it dangerous—so we did not even include it. By 1997, when we wrote *The Rules II,* there was a little more interest in online dating and we wrote a short chapter telling women the pitfalls of this chat-intensive dating method, how to best apply *The Rules,* and how to play it safe.

Back then, there were only a handful of dating websites. By 1999 there were more than 2,500 Internet sites devoted to matchmaking. And the numbers are still climbing worldwide.

Today, busy professional men and women think nothing of placing an ad and photo online and coming home every night to dozens of e-mails from desirable members of the opposite sex. They spend hours on the computer every day in online relationships or chat rooms or just answering their e-mail. The only problem is that online dating has become a little like a bad bar scene. Women are making serious mistakes in the way they meet and talk to men online. Women need to know:

- how to write effective ads
- how to answer e-mails
- how to act in chat rooms
- how to set boundaries with men online, and
- how to weed out the good guys from the bad.

And we're not just talking about women who use online dating services and chat rooms (an online forum where people can converse with each other by posting messages in real time). Today, virtually *everyone* uses e-mail; it's as common as a phone call. More men are simply asking women out or asking them about their day by e-mail instead of or in addition to calling, whether they first met these women through love@aol, personals. yahoo.com, or at a party at a friend's house. These days, men and women meeting for the first time often exchange e-mail addresses—sometimes before they exchange phone numbers!

Women meeting new men at business conferences, birthday parties, or clubs give out their e-mail addresses and also take men's e-mail addresses, and then find themselves in an e-mail relationship with a man. These women are just as prone to making the same mistakes online as women using online dating services and chat rooms—*mistakes that can ruin their relationships*.

E-mail courtship has made dating more hazardous than ever. With e-mail, women are tempted to let their guard down, let it all hang out, Instant Message men all night, and have cybersex (not *The Rules!*). But we believe you cannot e-mail with abandon, without thinking, without *Rules*. You must watch what you say, how often you say it, no matter what or how often he e-mails you, otherwise the relationship becomes so casual that it can go poof!—disappear—like a blank computer screen.

What many women don't realize is that an e-mail is just like a phone call—it does count! Women are making the same kind of mistakes online they make on the phone, mistakes that allow an e-courtship to become too easy. But these mistakes can be easily corrected with a set of *Rules* do's and don'ts. Hence *The Rules for Online Dating*. In this book, you will find out, among other things:

- Why you must let a man e-mail you first, regardless of how you met him
- Why not to answer men's ads
- How to create a good screen name or ad name
- The right way—and the wrong way—to write an online ad
- How and when to answer men's e-mails and Instant Messages
- How to do *The Rules* in any relationship that uses e-mail, no matter whether you first met online or offline

- How to prevent the relationship from becoming too casual
- How to not let online men waste your time
- How to set up the first face-to-face meeting with your e-mail guy ("date zero")
- How to evaluate the quality of an online relationship as it develops
- Potentially life-saving safety tips

You may be wondering at this point: If the premise of *The Rules* is that a man must pursue a woman and she must be mysterious and challenging, how is that premise going to work on an Internet dating website where you have to post a photo and describe yourself in an ad for all the world to see? You can definitely retain your mystery and keep yourself from being too available on dating websites and even in chat rooms. Read on, and we will tell you exactly how to apply the basic *Rules* premise to online and e-mail dating for the best possible results.

2

A Word to Online Dating Skeptics

We suspect that some of you may be reading this book only out of curiosity, still reluctant to actually try online dating. You may believe in *The Rules* all right, but you may not yet believe in online dating. You may not know anyone who is doing it or you may know one or two girlfriends who are, but neither has met Mr. Right. And even though you are meeting no one at all at clubs, parties, or through personal introductions, you just don't like the idea of meeting men online.

Or perhaps you think online dating is just for losers and men and women who have no social skills, desperate people who are forced to do this as a last resort. You may think that there is no way you can have any real chemistry with online profiles that are probably fabricated and photos that hardly resemble the person. You haven't yet tried it, but you are *sure* it wouldn't work for you. You would rather stay single than put your profile and photo up for friends, college roommates, coworkers, and neighbors to see. The whole idea of it makes you ill—even though some of these people may be online themselves!

We know how you feel.

Only a few years ago when we wrote *The Rules II,* we had nothing good to say about online dating. We thought it was potentially dangerous to meet with strangers. We also thought it would be hard for a man to feel a spark online in the same way he would meeting a woman in person, especially if the woman didn't post a photo. We thought that e-mailing back and forth endlessly, possibly for weeks or months, would ruin any chance for *Rules* mystery and challenge to happen.

But facts speak louder than words. Over the last few years, millions of men and women have joined online dating services and many women, especially those over the age of 30, are using online dating as their primary means of meeting men. They are not meeting men at work, as most of their coworkers and clients are married. They are too tired after a long day at work to go to a singles dance or a party. They don't have the time for a week at Club Med or a singles vacation. Or they don't have the money for video dating and matchmaking services, which typically charge thousands of dollars.

What are single men and women to do? We have come to believe online dating is the answer. It is effective, easy, inexpensive, and at your fingertips 24 hours a day.

But don't take our word for it. We are getting e-mails every day from women saying that they are meeting dozens of men a month that they would never normally meet in their work and social circles. And we have also heard from scores of men who say that they are using online dating because between work pressures, business travel, and sometimes children, they have no time to meet women at bars, parties, and in other conventional ways. They are finding online dating not only convenient, but effective.

"My life is as full as it can possibly be," explained David, a 42-year-old architect and father of three young boys. "I've a challenging career and kids from a marriage that just ended. I have no time to meet women any other way. A friend of mine met his wife online and said, try it, so here I am. I've met dozens of interesting women while looking for the right one. Online dating is perfect for me."

A doctor friend of ours in her thirties who went to a prestigious college and medical school used to spend her Saturday nights and Sunday afternoons with videos and potato chips. Kim recently e-mailed us that she has three dates with men she met online this weekend. An actress in her early fifties we know is booked all weekend with "date zeros"—the first face-to-face date with an e-mail correspondent—from men she met online. Sheila (not her real name) is as giddy about it as a teenager. Before posting her ad, she spent weekends alone at her country home with Danielle Steel novels.

Others have e-mailed us to say they have been in actual relationships for several months with men they first met on the Internet. And some have even reported that they are now engaged to these men, some of whom live on the other side of the country and even overseas!

Are you looking for another social outlet? If the answer is yes, we encourage you to put aside your pride and prejudice until you have tried online dating for a few months—or even a year—and see for yourself. You have nothing to lose, and all you need to start is a computer and a scanned photo!

Maybe you are not computer literate. Maybe you don't even

own a computer. Maybe you can't afford a computer right now. We have had friends in your position. Don't let this stop you. We were happy to post ads and photos for our friends and answer their mail until they were ready to buy their own computer—and one of them just got engaged to a man who answered her ad. So ask a friend or coworker to do the same for you. We are sure you have friends who would be happy to help you out. Just make a beginning—baby steps—by posting your ad and photo with only one website dating service. Good luck!

Ellen and Sherrie

3

An Online Consultation
Success Story

Courtney, 32, an attractive editor at a fashion magazine, called us for a consultation. She was at her wits' end about her two-year relationship with Glen, 44, a handsome photographer she met at a friend's birthday party. Glen walked over to her, spoke to her first, and asked for her number before she left. He called the next day and asked her out for the coming weekend. So far, so good. But Courtney, who had only skimmed *The Rules* once in a bookstore and thought "I don't need this," then proceeded to break every *Rule*. She saw Glen all the time and e-mailed and called him as often as he e-mailed and called her. She slept with him on the second date, invited him to her office Christmas party, and took him as her date to her cousin's wedding before he did anything comparable.

After two years, Glen had said "I love you" only once when he was drunk, and nothing about exclusivity or the future. Both had been engaged once before, but never married. Glen said his parents' divorce devastated him and he was leery of marriage. For their two-year anniversary, Courtney cooked a romantic dinner but the evening ended disastrously with Courtney complaining to Glen that he was "not going forward in their relationship" and even "pulling back a little."

After that conversation, Glen's e-mails were less frequent and sprinkled with words such as "confused," and "needing more space." He didn't ask her out for the next two weeks. When she found out through a mutual friend that he had been out on Saturday night with his ex-girlfriend Fiona, a leggy 29-year-old model, Courtney called him up at work and blew her fuse. That's when Glen told her "that's it, you're crowding me, we're through." The next day Courtney called us, heartbroken and in tears.

We told her that although Glen had initially approached her—an auspicious, *Rules*-y beginning for a relationship—she'd broken so many *Rules* after that that he lost interest. The only solution for her was to leave him alone and only see him again if he showed up with a ring and a wedding date. "No contact at all?" Courtney asked in disbelief.

"No contact," we said. "Besides, we don't think he is calling you any time soon. If he really loved you and wanted to be with you, he would have said that his ex meant nothing to him, and he'd have tried to patch things up with you. Instead, he broke up with you. Sounds like he is not in love with you at all. So if you are smart, you won't sit by the phone waiting. Why don't you take some social actions? How about putting up an ad with your photo online and meeting new men that way? It will be easier not to call Glen if you are busy reading adoring e-mails from men who like your photo. Just do the online dating *Rules*. Maybe you will meet your husband this way."

Courtney's answer was: "I don't want to go online. Everyone knows me out here; I'm a fashion editor, I'm the first to wear all the designer clothes. I'd be so embarrassed if anyone saw my photo on the Internet. Besides, I don't want to meet anyone else; I just want Glen."

We told her, "Do it anyway."

One month later, Courtney called us again to say that Glen had left her a message just to say hello, and she wanted to know if she could call him back. We said definitely not. A week later, she forwarded to us an e-mail from Glen, saying, "Your not returning my call tells me that you are not committed to this relationship or me, which is why I had to stray in the first place. You are the one giving me mixed messages. You want to move forward but you didn't call me back!"

Again, we told Courtney not to respond, that he was playing mind games with her and trying to blame her for the breakup, that he was insincere, and not planning to marry her anyway.

Sure enough, one month later, Courtney called us to say that Glen e-mailed her, "No need to write back. I am living with Fiona and we are talking about getting married. I guess I should thank you. Good-bye and good luck." Talk about what would have been a roller-coaster relationship!

Courtney continued to call us to talk about Glen and to ask if there was anything she could do to get him back. "He must love me if he e-mailed me that. Maybe he's trying to make me jealous!"

We told her it didn't appear that way, so next! We also told her that the next time she called us, it couldn't be about Glen, but about the ad and photo she posted online and the online *Rules* she was doing. Reluctantly, she agreed to place an ad that day, although she continued to think about Glen 24/7 and thought she would just do "this online thing" to keep busy until he came to his senses and begged her to come back.

Gradually, Courtney began to enjoy online dating. Part of her was relieved that she could meet men on the computer in the comfort of her home while wearing sweatpants, no makeup, and a ponytail. Being as upset as she was over Glen, she had no interest in going to parties or being out there anyway, at least for the time being.

We helped Courtney come up with the screen name FashionableNFun32 and helped her choose an attractive, smiling photo of herself to post with her ad. She received more than 100 responses in the first month. Following *The Rules,* she weeded out responses that sounded inappropriate; either they sounded too sexual, or as if they were written by married men, or by 25-year-olds looking for an older woman, or by other "time-wasters." Courtney agreed to wait 24 hours after receiving each e-mail and then to answer only those e-mails that remained after she'd screened out the inappropriate ones— e-mails that looked as if they were written by nice, attractive men. No more *Rule*-breaking for her! After finding her first few dates to be disappointing—the guys were great on the computer, but boring or not attractive to her in person—Courtney called us to say she was discouraged. "Are you sure this online thing works?" she said. "What if all of them are nothing like their ads?"

We told her to keep trying, to put up another ad on another service, and to also go to singles parties, or activities like skiing, to meet men in person as well.

Three months later, Courtney e-mailed us that she thought she had met a great catch, and asked us to go over every e-mail correspondence between them as well as their dates to make sure she didn't blow it. "It's always the ones I like that I get in trouble with," she said.

DannyDJ41, a disc jockey at a popular radio station in the same city, e-mailed Courtney when he saw her photo and ad on the dating website, "Are you beautiful or what? Just my type. Can we chat sometime online?" By that, Danny meant he wanted to Instant Message Courtney.

An Instant Message, popularly known as an IM, is a message that pops up on your online computer screen in real time, and to which you can respond in real time and create a dialog back and forth. With an IM, a man knows if and when you're on the computer and can get you into a conversation in an instant if you respond. Courtney knew from consulting with us that Instant Message exchanges were too casual and—even worse—can lead some women into *Rules*-breaking Instant Message marathons that last for hours. We advise women not to answer IMs so that they will not appear so easy to get ahold of. (You can also activate "blocking" online, a feature that prevents others from knowing if and when you're online and blocks IMs from reaching you.)

Courtney looked up DannyDJ41's profile, thought he was really cute, but did not want to take him up on his invitation to "chat sometime online" via Instant Messages. So she waited 24 hours to e-mail him back, "Thanks, but my schedule is kind of crazy, different everyday . . ." hoping this answer would persuade him to e-mail her back, rather than send her an Instant Message. Trying again to get Courtney to make herself available for an Instant Message exchange, DannyDJ41 answered, via regular e-mail: "Well, I'll try you later tonight." Meanwhile, Courtney blocked herself from receiving Instant Messages.

Two days passed and no word from Danny. Courtney feared Danny may have poofed!—disappeared after his first two e-mails—and she was seriously tempted to unblock herself.

On the third day, he e-mailed her: "Was looking for you the last couple of nights. Are you ever online?"

It was clear Danny had been trying to Instant Message Courtney the previous two nights, but hadn't been able to catch her online. FashionableNFun32 e-mailed him back 24 hours later: "Sorry, got home late the last two nights, work parties."

DannyDJ41 sent her back an e-mail (not an Instant Message, but an e-mail) five seconds later: "Sounds like a great job, what do you do? Maybe we can go out one night and talk about it. Are you free on the weekends?"

FashionableNFun32, 24 hours later: "Hi, Danny. Yes, I love my job. I'm a fashion editor for a magazine, it's great. Sure, I can be free on the weekends."

DannyDJ41, an hour later after his radio show: "Great, here's my number, can I have your number?"

FashionableNFun32 did not call his phone number, but, instead, sent him an e-mail 24 hours later with her phone number: "My cell is 555-6219." She knew that he—not she—had to be the one to call.

Danny called Courtney the next day and asked if she wanted to meet for drinks, lunch, or dinner. "Drinks sound great," she replied, knowing that less is always better.

They made plans for drinks that Friday night at 6 P.M. On the date, Danny looked and sounded even better than his ad. He was very cute, smart, and witty and they laughed a lot. Courtney didn't want the evening to end, but she knew she would abide by *The Rules* and pull herself away an hour and a half later. She glanced at her watch every so often just to make sure she didn't lose track of time. They talked about work, movies, music, and other general topics until Danny asked the question she dreaded most, "So why has a pretty girl like you never been married?"

Courtney breathed, counted to five and with a big smile said, "I haven't really thought about it."

We had taught Courtney that taking a few seconds to pause was helpful as it creates space between your thoughts and what you want to say and makes you seem less eager. In addition, we told her she never had to answer any questions she didn't feel like answering or that made her feel uncomfortable.

Pre-*Rules,* she would have breathlessly told him about her previous engagement and how she thought she was going to marry Glen, but then Glen went back to his ex-girlfriend Fiona, etc., and she would have asked him the same question back, and a whole relationship talk about exes and feelings and regrets would have gone on. It would have been too many drinks and too many hours—far too much for date zero. Instead, she smiled and sipped her drink. After an hour and a half, she looked at her watch and said, "This has been nice, but I really have to get going . . ."

Danny looked startled, as if no woman had ever ended a date with him so quickly before.

"Are you sure you have to go? I was thinking we could grab a bite . . ."

"Thanks, but I have an early morning phone conference tomorrow and I have to prepare."

"Can I see you again?" he asked.

Courtney waited, counting to five, then said, "Sure."

She called us that night to report that *The Rules* worked like a charm, and also to say that she hadn't thought about Glen once that night, which was a miracle in itself. Courtney asked if it would be okay to e-mail Danny, "Thanks for the drink and I can't wait to hear your show," but we told her no, her thank-you e-mail would show too much interest. It was his pleasure to take her out. Besides, we told her, he's a popular DJ; many women would have slept with him already. Courtney listened to us and did not e-mail Danny.

When she turned on her computer the next morning, she was glad she hadn't. Danny had e-mailed her, "Had a great time last night. You are even prettier in person and so much fun to talk to. Are you free again this Saturday night? Would you like to go to dinner and a movie?" Courtney waited 24 hours and responded: "I had a nice time, too. Saturday sounds great."

Danny began to ask Courtney out at the end of dates, or by phone, or by e-mail. She was light and breezy on dates and always ended them first. She did not mention Glen by name, but said that she had been in a relationship that "didn't work out," and although she opened up a little bit more with Danny after each date, she did not indulge in any heavy relationship talk. After she felt comfortable with Danny and knew she would hear from him again, she slept with him without initiating any "Where is this going now?" talk. Of course, he brought it up. He called her the next day and asked her to take down her ad, saying he was hoping they could be exclusive. Courtney agreed. He bought her earrings for her birthday and roses for Valentine's Day.

Courtney was in heaven, except for one thing. She said Danny e-mailed her about three times a week with a "Hi, thinking of you" or a joke but only called once or twice a week to confirm their date. "I e-mail him back once a week. Am I doing something wrong? Glen used to call every day, sometimes twice a day," she said. "Should I tell Danny I prefer to talk on the phone?"

"No," we told her. "E-mail and phone are the same thing; as long as he is asking you out every week, leave it alone." We reminded her that Glen didn't marry her, and that calls are not necessarily indicative of a man's feelings.

After that we did not hear from Courtney for six months and we hoped that she was not breaking any *Rules* or that Danny had not poofed! Then just before New Year's, she called to say that Danny proposed by sending her an e-mail with pasted flowers and a ring and the message "Have a surprise for you tonight."

That night over a candlelit dinner, he popped the question and she said yes.

The next day Courtney called us to say, "Thanks for making me go online! I never would have done it on my own. Now all my friends are doing it! I love being a success story."

4

Be an Online "CUAO"

In our first book, we coined the term "Creature Unlike Any Other" to describe the essence of a *Rules* girl. A CUAO is a state of mind, an attitude. You don't have to be born with it—it can be learned and practiced.

To be a CUAO, you don't have to be the prettiest or the smartest (whew!) to feel good about yourself. In fact, it doesn't matter if you have 30 pounds to lose or never finished college, you just think you are enough. You act confident, you hold your head up high, you don't worry about the competition. More than that, you realize there is no competition because you are unique—a Creature Unlike Any Other. You don't concern yourself with what other women are doing or not doing, particularly *Rules*-breakers. You feel that any man would be lucky to have you. You are not a snob, you just like yourself. And if you are at a time in your life when you don't really like yourself that much, you act as if!

You walk into a room with a spring in your step as if you just

got out of a limo. You smile a lot, you don't talk too much—
that shows nervousness and desperation and a bit of selfishness
since you're not allowing the other person to speak. Your ges-
tures are feminine, you would never ask a man out, go Dutch,
or ask where the relationship is going in the first six months.
You would never send a thank-you note after a date, you just
thank him at the end of the evening. After all, taking you out is
his pleasure. You always end the date first.

We know what you are probably thinking, "How am I to be
a CUAO if I am (gasp!) posting my photo and an ad on the
Internet? I mean, everyone is going to recognize my picture
and know I'm looking for a relationship. How hard-to-get can I
look, I mean, come on!"

We know what you mean. You are embarrassed about the
whole thing, but at the same time, you are single and you want
to find someone. And simply posting an ad on the Internet isn't
enough; you need to post your picture as well, because physical
attraction is so important.

So you're kind of stuck! You need to be in it to win it and,
like it or not, this is one of the more popular avenues for meeting men today. But how can a CUAO sign on an Internet dating website without feeling she is saying, "Hi, I'm desperate
and I have not met anyone so now I am using the Internet to
meet men"?

Relax! Posting an ad in itself is *not* desperate. It's simply like
walking into a singles dance or a bar—everyone is there for the
same reason, to meet someone. There is no shame in this, so
don't think you can't post an ad or your photo because everyone will find out you are looking for a relationship. For all you
know, your next-door neighbor or coworker is looking for a
relationship online as well.

The trick is to write your ad so it doesn't reek of desperation. You should write it in a nonchalant way so that it looks like you did it on your lunch hour, or you did it because your friend put you up to it, as if you just heard that this is a good way to meet men. Make it sound light and casual—just the latest, fashionable thing to do. Don't we all wear crazy clothes sometimes just because everybody's doing it? Don't we go on crazy diets just to lose weight?

Well, the best way to make Internet dating look like nothing more than just another interesting venue to meet men—as opposed to some drastic act of desperation—is to write your ad as something quick and easy to read, flip and interesting, without giving away too much information, yet looking as if you have said it all.

Hence, don't take Internet dating service questionnaires too seriously; don't even answer every question, particularly deep questions about your five-year goals and your soul mate (see *Rule 3:* "Less Is More When Writing Your Ad"). No matter how much the dating service questionnaires probe, you should give simple one- or two-sentence answers. Remember, you are a CUAO, your life is full and exciting, you don't have much time for this. So when a questionnaire asks you what you are looking for ("to meet new people," "to date," "a long-term relationship," "marriage"), you should give the answer that shows the least involvement ("to meet new people") as you barely know what you are having for dinner tonight, much less what sort of relationship you want—even if you are in therapy three times a week to deal with just that issue!

If you are a CUAO doing online dating, you put up a short ad with a pretty picture and let men e-mail you. You never answer men's ads—that's chasing men; CUAOs let men e-mail them first. Offline, the rule is the same: If you meet a man at a party and exchange cards, you don't e-mail him first, just as you wouldn't call him first either. You wait until he contacts you, or not. Once a man has e-mailed you, you wait 24 hours to answer his e-mail. Anything sooner reeks of desperation. Your e-mails are short and sweet. You don't argue with men, say anything negative ("dating sucks!" "men are jerks!"), or go on and on about your problems. You are only available to men on the computer at normal "business" hours, not after midnight and *never* on weekends. CUAOs are either booked all weekend or they make it look as if they're booked by blocking themselves online. Even if you're home on a Saturday night, you block yourself from receiving Instant Messages on the computer so that men cannot catch you sitting at home on date night.

As a CUAO, you don't travel to meet a man. Men must come to you. You don't waste time on men who are casual about you. It's next! for them. A CUAO values her time, so no long e-mail exchanges or pen-pal relationships for her.

A CUAO does not get discouraged that there are no men out there and then feels she must therefore bend *The Rules* to snag somebody. She trusts that the man of her dreams, whether offline or on, is out there and that all she has to do is follow *The Rules* and be patient.

Although you may be sitting at your computer in sweatpants responding to e-mails, you are still a CUAO. If you imagine yourself in high heels and a sleek outfit, your makeup on perfectly, and your hair blown out like a magazine model's, your writing will reflect this. As a CUAO, you should never feel desperate. Know in your heart that any man would be lucky to read your ad and even luckier to have your e-mail address. Answer the dating service questionnaire as if a limousine is outside waiting to take you somewhere and you really don't have a lot of time. When the form asks what your hobbies are, you barely have time to type out "reading, dancing, and skiing." The limo is waiting!

THE RULES FOR ONLINE DATING

Rule 1

Don't Answer Men's Ads or E-mail Them First

The three basic premises of this book and all our *Rules* books are: A man must initially feel a spark for a woman; the man must pursue the woman; and all men love a challenge. If you are answering a man's ad, you are not using any of these premises. To answer a man's ad is, in effect, to tell *him* that you feel a spark, that you chose him from scores of other men, that he is absolutely your type, that you like his killer abs or his dazzling smile or his philosophy on life. Answering a man's ad is to pursue a man; it's no different from approaching a man at a party or bar, calling him, and asking him out. He knows you like him and the challenge is over. What's worse, since he didn't approach you first, he didn't necessarily feel that same spark for you.

Answering a man's ad, e-mailing, or Instant Messaging him first or even e-mailing a man first whom you met at the company picnic doesn't work because you are the aggressor. You are initiating the whole scenario. If he does end up dating you, you'll never know if he's dating you because it's easy and convenient for him to do so, or because he's really crazy about you. After all, he didn't search through dozens of profiles, love your smile, and answer your ad, or e-mail you first after you exchanged business cards at a party or work seminar.

We have found that women who answer men's ads or e-mail them first—even if they end up dating these men—have more problems than women who follow *The Rules.* Sometimes these men skip weeks here and there in asking you out, or skip important dates like Valentine's Day, or they cancel dates, or just never commit.

Whenever we get e-mails from women saying they e-mailed him first or answered his ad, we think, uh-oh, as there are invariably problems: He takes months to ask for her phone number or to meet her. He expects her to visit him ("Work is busy, can't get away, you'll love Boston"). He keeps his ad up. He won't commit. He forgets her birthday. He has ex-girlfriends or an ex-wife that he still sees inappropriately. He tells her he feels smothered and wants space.

We know what you are thinking! No one you like is answering your ad and you just found a guy's profile that is simply too good to be true. He is definitely your type in every way, you like the same things, and he is adorable. You just have to answer his ad!

Or you met a guy at a party, it was a group thing, and you exchanged e-mail addresses, and you think what could be the harm in e-mailing him first? After all, it's not a phone call, it seems harmless enough.

We recently did a consultation with Lauren, an attractive 35-year-old attorney for a TV network in Los Angeles. She told us that she moved to LA from New York because her dream was to work in television. She was also looking for "a change of scenery" because her two-year relationship to a guy she lived with had recently ended badly when he decided not to marry her. She said she was lonely in LA for many months, working 12-hour days and meeting no one. Most of the other lawyers at her company were married with children.

Then a coworker told her about online dating and she thought that might be her answer. She posted an ad with her photo on a couple of services, but found that most of the men in LA who responded to her ad were not on her professional level; instead, they were "actor/waiters and surfer types." That's when she decided to "take matters into her own hands" and answer an ad or two to increase her chances of meeting Mr. Right.

After a quick search in the 35–45 category, she settled on TVExec38, who was not only cute and in her field, but an East Coast transplant as well! Lauren e-mailed him: "Hi, I like your ad . . . we have a lot in common. I also work for one of the networks and just moved here from New York."

TVExec38 seemed friendly enough, he even responded the same day: "Hi, welcome to LA. My name is Steve, I write for a sitcom . . ."

They e-mailed each other about ten times, chatting about everything from their favorite shows, to the differences between NY and LA restaurants, to the weather, before Steve asked her out for drinks. Lauren was walking on air when she met Steve as he was not only good-looking but smart, charismatic, and athletic as well. Steve thought Lauren, a petite brunette, was cute, but not exactly his type as he liked tall blondes. Nevertheless he enjoyed her company and continued to ask her out every week, although often at the last minute. On their fifth date, they had sex, and all Steve said afterward was "Well, let's get together again. I'll call you or you call me . . ."

When Steve didn't call for a few days, Lauren called him to ask if everything was okay or if maybe he was pulling back because they had slept together. "No, just have a lot on my mind. I don't know if I told you but I'm selling my condo and buying a house and it's very complicated. I'll call you when things settle down."

"No problem," Lauren said, trying to be cool, but dying inside. She knew deep down inside that when a guy really likes you he calls the day after sex. But she told herself this house thing was a big investment, that anyone would be preoccupied, and she tried not to mind that he was buying a new house and not even asking for her input.

After that, Steve skipped a week here or there, usually calling Lauren Saturday afternoon for Saturday night dates. He always had a good reason for calling her at the last minute: work was crazy, he didn't know if he would be called in for last-minute rewrites, and so on. Lauren was always on hold, but she told herself it was OK and she always accepted. Once Steve even canceled a last-minute date at the last second, saying he hurt his leg at the gym and wanted to stay home, take Advil, and watch TV. When he didn't invite her over to join him, she asked if there was anything she could bring him, hoping he would get the hint. He didn't. "That's sweet, but no thanks," he replied. "Talk to you next week. I'll call you or you call me . . ."

When Lauren didn't hear from him by Wednesday, she called him pretending to be interested in his leg, but really wanting to find out what was going on between them. "I haven't seen you in two weeks. Is something wrong?"

"No, the truth is, I'm just not interested in a girlfriend right now. I know I put up an ad but I wasn't looking for anything serious. I think you're great and we can still see each other once in a while. I'll call you or you call me . . ."

Lauren called us instead and we told her not to bother. She didn't call him and he didn't call her and that was the end of their relationship. It took Lauren two months to get over Steve, but she learned her lesson and never answered another man's ad. (Steve's ad is still up!)

Unfortunately, Lauren's experience is typical. It almost always results in heartache when you answer a man's ad.

Ditto for e-mail *Rule*-breaking. Allison, 25, and her friends met a group of guys at the beach. They all hung out, ate ice cream, played Frisbee, and at the end of the day they exchanged e-mail addresses. Everyone said, "We really have to do this again!"

Allison thought one of the guys, Steven, 27, was just her type. She e-mailed him early Monday morning, "Hi, I think you need Frisbee lessons! LOL" Of course, he was more than happy to e-mail her two hours later with, "Depends on who the teacher is, want to get together?" It was fast and furious on- and offline for two months. She broke every *Rule.* By the third month, he started calling and e-mailing less and finally ended things with "Sorry, but work is just crazy and I can't focus on a relationship right now."

A woman who has been doing online dating for several years confirms our theory: "I would have to say that the guys I wrote to first definitely did not work out as often as the guys who wrote to me first. In fact, I would say 100 percent of the guys who became my boyfriends wrote to me first. If I wrote to them first it never really went too far. Alas, why do *The Rules* have to be so true?"

You may be wondering if there are any exceptions to this rule. Yes, in very rare cases we have heard about a woman or two who answered a man's ad, then did all the other online dating *Rules* we suggest in this book, and they are now happily married. How so? According to these women, the men they were dating said that coincidentally they had seen the women's ads and were going to answer them after their MBA exam or the Super Bowl, but the women beat them to the punch.

You may not be so lucky, so we still don't suggest you take a chance and answer men's ads and risk getting very hurt. If you want to take risks, may we suggest that you gamble $100 at a blackjack table before you ever answer a man's ad.

Rule 2

Create a Good Screen Name

A good screen name is important because, other than your photo, your screen name is all a man has to go by when he scans ads or enters a chat room, searching for his type. It should not be boring, but it should not be too sexy either. You do not want a man to skip over your ad because it is either too ho-hum or too marriage-minded, nor do you want to go to the opposite extreme and attract men who are interested in just sex or married men looking for cybersex. Strive for something in the middle.

A good screen name is written in initial capital letters, is eye-catching, and also helps men zone in on what they are looking for by being descriptive and factual, giving hair color, height, or age. Examples of good screen and ad names:

- BlondBeauty50 (gives look and age)
- PetiteBrunette34, TrulyCute22, GorgeousGreenEyez44 (descriptive, cute, and not overdone)

Bad screen and ad names:

- Intoxicating35 (too sexual)
- YouWon'tBeDisappointed (aside from being pompous, says nothing specific about looks)
- LaughterLuvSerenity (too general and saccharine, save it for a bumper sticker)
- Nanci42 (says nothing about looks)
- LookinForLuv, SeriousGrlNow, LookinForMySoulmate, SweetGirlSeeksMr.Right (all of these are too intense, too marriage-minded, and sure to scare men away)

If at all possible, use a separate screen name for online dating. Try not to use a work screen name such as susanjones@adwear.com because it identifies your real name and workplace, and if you mess up on responding or get a little too familiar with a "great guy" and tell him personal stuff about yourself, do you really want to be identifiable if he turns out to be a creep and forwards your e-mail all over the place?

Also do not write anything obscure or anything that requires too much work to decipher. You will attract no one. For example, an English major/literary agent ran an ad with the name MaggieNadia. For the few men who bothered to read the ad, it said: "This is how Jack Nicholson once described Jessica Lange and I think that image suits me to a tee: a classic chassis (sturdy) combined with a delicate and wide-eyed vulnerability. I only wish I had written that line myself. . . ."

Very interesting, but who cares?

Men are not looking for Shakespeare or Hemingway when they browse on Matchmaker.com. They are looking for a picture they find attractive and a fun description. They don't want to work that hard. And when they think you are working too hard on an ad, they think, "Uh-oh, what is wrong with her that she is trying so hard?" So don't try to be so original or poetic, just be as light and breezy as you can.

Another esoteric screen name is CuriousGrrl2002 and begins like this: "Do you believe in an afterlife? Or do you believe that only today matters and why live for some dubious tomorrow?"

This would give any man a headache.

Remember, they are looking for women they are attracted to who are psychologically stable, so don't go nuts on them.

You know those cover lines on *Cosmo* and *Glamour* magazines, such as "Flat Stomach in 7 Days," and "Cellulite-Buster—10 Minutes a Day," and so on? Well, that's what your screen name and writing should be like. Catchy and easy.

Rule 3

Less Is More When Writing Your Ad

To join an online dating service, whether it is jdate.com, match.com, or love@aol, you are required to fill out a questionnaire that may include as many as 50 questions. This questionnaire essentially makes up your ad or profile. Questions may include height, weight, job description, favorite TV show, goals, ideals, and a self-description.

Do not agonize over filling out these forms, since most men will only look at your photo and simply scan whatever you write. Do not feel you have to answer every question and do not break any *Rules* in doing so.

A peculiar phenomenon born of online dating has occurred whereby, for some reason, women who would never consider responding to such intimate questions on a date or in a bar will answer very personal questions with honesty and integrity in beautifully scripted essays about things that are absolutely nobody's business such as "five-year goals" and "annual income." We believe a man has to go out with you for several *months* to find out what your goals are! So less is more on these forms.

Thus, the key to writing a good ad is to give the impression that you just threw some answers down with a cute pic on your way out to a business meeting or the gym, because, after all, you are very busy. Write it like you have lots of things going on in your life, but that you just thought this would be fun. Do not put a lot of effort into it as if you are writing your doctoral thesis. You should reveal very little about yourself so that they have to ask you out on a date to find out more.

Here is an example of a good *Rules*-y ad, titled BlueEyedBlondBeauty32:

I live in Boston. I'm 32 years old, 5'6", 115 pounds.
I am single. I like hiking, skiing, and dancing.
I work in Advertising, have a BA in Marketing.
I am fun, sophisticated yet easygoing.
I like Chinese and Italian food.
I'd like to meet someone who is between the ages of 32 and 40.

Tell us about yourself: *Let's see, I like to go to the movies, ski, or just hang out with friends.*

What is your perfect match? *Someone kind, honest, smart, with a good sense of humor.*

What sort of first dates do you enjoy? *Pleasant ones. You click. It is not work. You are not looking at your watch, hoping it would end. You leave feeling good.*

What sort of relationship are you looking for? *One where it's just "easy," you truly enjoy being with that person and he with you, it just feels great!*

The reason that this is a good ad is that it is factual (height, weight, and other physical attributes) and it is easy to read, not poetic or heavy-handed or demanding. Nothing about intense feelings, longings, hopes, and dreams that would scare the average man away. She does not say she is looking for marriage and children. She is just looking to meet someone nice for dinner or a movie. She does not reveal her hand.

We looked at hundreds of ads on several services and many were too long, too deep, and too demanding. Classic mistakes we found included:

1. Women who say they are looking for love and marriage and children or describing themselves as marriage-minded. Although it is obvious that this is why most people are online, you are putting all your cards on the table to say so. What mystery or challenge is there if you are telling a man you haven't even met yet what your plans are? He will feel suffocated before the relationship even begins. Just say you are looking for a date or to meet new people, so he can relax and breathe.

2. Women who say they are "willing or open to relocating." You have not even met these men yet and you are already packing your bags, yanking your kids out of elementary school, and selling your house. You sound too eager, like a used-car salesman lowering his price before getting an offer. When he proposes with a ring and a wedding date, you can talk about relocating, not in your ad.

3. Women who post more than one ad on the same dating website. It looks desperate and doesn't work. Trust us, if he passed over your first ad, he is not going to be

interested in another version of you. A man either likes your type or he doesn't. Changing your screen name and your pose is not going to do the trick. This is not like bingo, where you can increase your chances of winning by playing two boards. There is an attraction or there isn't. So the rule is: Post different ads on *different* sites, but never post more than one ad on the same site.

4. Women who post three or more photos in the same ad. One photo is enough. When you start posting a headshot, you on the beach, and you out to dinner with friends in the same ad, you start to look desperate. A man needs just one good headshot to see if he wants to go out with you.

5. Women who write long answers with tons of feelings that look like they were written by Hallmark or right after a therapy session.

Too many intense feelings scare men away. When asked to describe the ideal relationship, one attractive woman in her forties answered:

I want a relationship like Susan Sarandon and Tim Robbins, a bond that is stronger than a piece of paper. Now that I am divorced, I know that a marriage certificate isn't as important as a life-long commitment.

This is too much. Always remember, you are writing this on your way out. You are not analyzing celebrity relationships and asking men to be movie stars. You are not putting down marriage. You are not cynical. You are happy and optimistic.

When asked to describe her ideal mate, one successful woman in her thirties answered:

The man I want to meet is successful in business, sophisticated yet laid back, compassionate yet driven, outdoorsy but a homebody, who can take me to fine restaurants and on wonderful vacations, and most important be my best friend.

Is there anything she left out? Basically she is saying she wants everything, particularly a rich guy. She comes across as a gold digger.

When asked about life goals, one stunning woman in her fifties answered:

I am looking to share love and life. The joy is in the journey . . . discovering each other and embracing life. I am on the road a lot for my job so I want to know there is someone there for me when I come home . . . someone caring, honest, intelligent, a good listener. I want a man who is comfortable enough to let me see his inner child, someone not afraid to show his emotions. I'm ready to make a life-long commitment to the right person . . . .

This is not an answer to a question, it is poetry and therapy. Would you ever get on a microphone in a bar and read this aloud? We hope not.

Remember, you are talking to strangers! There is absolutely no mystery or excitement for a man when a woman says everything on her mind. It is also a burden for the average man to be told he must be Deepak Chopra in the relationship department. Besides, who *doesn't* want someone kind, loving, compassionate and so on? If you scan women's ads on the Internet, you will see that every woman wants the same thing!

Asked to describe one's physical attributes, another attractive woman in her thirties answered: "I have an infectious smile." We think this is too much. Be humble. Don't hype yourself. Let a man judge for himself when he sees your photo. Let a man say your smile is infectious or dazzling or whatever he thinks. Nothing is less attractive than an overblown ego.

Conversely, we have come across ads that don't do a woman justice. One 32-year-old woman who contacted us wanted to post an ad that said she got her "smile from her grandma Millie" and she admired "selfless souls like Mother Teresa," descriptions which we did not think would make men jump to e-mail her! After consulting with us and redoing her head shot to make herself look more youthful, she was able to truthfully change her ad to say that she looked "like *Titanic* actress Kate Winslet" and that she admired "selfless people like the late Princess Di, who was active in charity work."

Asked to describe a perfect date, another attractive woman in her forties answered:

> *Where we're not aware of the hours flying by . . . where neither of us wants to say good night, where neither of us needs to say good night.*

This woman is implying that she is run by her emotions. She is also implying that she would spend the night and maybe even have sex on the first date. A *Rules* girl always ends date zero first, usually after an hour or two, even if she is having a great time—especially if she is having a great time!—so he asks her out again.

If you read men's ads, you will see that they also write like women do, but they do so because they think that this is what women like to read. They know they can get you interested in them by saying "Communication is the key to a successful relationship," when in fact men hate to talk about relationships and would much prefer watching a football game with a bag of chips. So don't believe everything you read. Their ideal relationship is a lot of sex and fun and they don't take online dating questionnaires as seriously as women do. In fact, one real honest guy wrote in response to the question, "What have you learned from past relationships?," "I've learned that red goes with meat and white goes with chicken."

In answer to what you learned from past relationships, you can say something very neutral or vague like, "I think we mature from every relationship . . ." but nothing too serious like, "I've learned you have to communicate and work on your issues and never go to bed angry." Also, if the questionnaire asks for your five-year plan, do not say "to meet my soul mate, settle down, get married, and have kids." Too much, even if it's the truth. Just say "Thinking about today for now!" or even "I haven't really thought about it." Let him ask you out to find out more.

Here are some more pitfalls to avoid in online ads:

1. It is perfectly fine to leave a question blank, particularly embarrassing or negative questions, such as, "Why did your last relationship end?" or "What habits of others annoy you?"

2. Do not use the questionnaire as a way to hint to men to ask you out. For example, if a questionnaire asks about your favorite movies or political orientation, do not say, "Would love to talk about it over lunch" or "You'll have to ask

me on a date to find out." Just answer the question. If you are doing *The Rules,* you will be talking about work, hobbies, current events, and movies on your lunch dates anyway.

3. If a questionnaire asks for your income, check off "not available" or "none of your business." Your finances are not his business. If you make a lot of money and say so, how do you know if men are e-mailing you because they want a rich girlfriend? You want them to like you for you, not your money.

4. In the section where you are asked to describe yourself, if there is a multiple choice, check "cheerful," not "romantic." Romantic is too intense. He can fill out romantic or whatever he wants, but as a *Rules* girl, you shouldn't. In answer to the question why are you joining an online service, check "My friend put me up to it" or "Curious" if at all possible, not "Hoping to meet someone." (Checking "Hoping to meet someone" is not the end of the world, but it is obvious, so why say it?)

5. If the form asks what question do you have for men, don't say, "Are you looking for a serious relationship?" or "Do you like children?" Ask something neutral, like "What are your hobbies?"

6. Remember, shorter is better as men are more apt to read an ad that does not go on and on. No home pages or biographies, please. And no philosophical dissertations. Do not go on and on about how you are a romantic person hoping to find love and laughter with the right partner. Do not say, as one woman did, "I believe in love because that's the most important thing in life and even though I am

divorced, I am not bitter and still believe in happily-ever-after with the right person, maybe you? Let's give love a second chance." You will scare men away with such intensity.

7. Don't be demanding with lists of non-negotiables. Some women make wish lists in their ads, such as the following:

> "I am looking to date men with advanced degrees, professionals only, doctors, lawyers, management types."
> "I would like men with incomes over $100,000."
> "Don't answer this ad if you are not serious."
> "I don't respond to Instant Messages if you don't e-mail me first."
> "I don't respond to e-mails with no photos."
> "I don't date men who are separated; you must be divorced."
> "I don't date men who are five years younger, so don't bother to respond."
> "I don't date men who don't disclose their job and income."
> "This is what I require . . ."
> "I am looking for a man who acts like a man . . ."
> "I don't play games . . ."
> "No game-players, please . . ."
> "I am a passionate woman . . ."

and so forth.

To be so brazenly specific in your ad is neither *Rules*-y nor refined. These wish lists don't work anyway, as most men will respond to whatever ad they like and the men these women are actually seeking out will be turned off by these opportunistic requests. Sure, you can say you want someone who shares your passion for hiking or the like, but to say you only want a certain profession (management types, doctors, lawyers, or men who make over $100,000) makes you look like you are too intensely hunting for prey. It's like walking into a bar and saying "Who in this room will buy me a three-carat ring with a Tiffany setting?" It's too much, too calculated, not humble, and has little to do with chemistry or love.

It would be nice if finding a partner was like ordering a sweater from an L.L. Bean catalog, but it isn't. So we suggest you just put up your best pic with a light, breezy, nonchalant ad that is not too demanding. Whoever responds, responds. Then just date whomever you like.

So, less is more! However, if the dating service will not accept a low word count, or if they tell you that you must write more, then write the absolute minimum number of words.

Do not think, as some women do, that if you don't answer every question about marriage and personal goals men will think you are not serious. Most men know you joined the service to meet and find a boyfriend or husband. That's the one thing you don't have to tell them!

Rule 4

Post a Smiling Photo

Your photo is not just a part of your ad, it is everything! Any normal guy thinks a woman is trying to hide something if she doesn't post her photo. And can you blame him? What guy is going to go up to a woman at a party if she has a bag over her head? A great ad, even with a good screen name, is just not enough. If you want a real *Rules* (spark first) relationship, it's better to have a picture up.

Besides, as we have noted before, men don't really read ads, they look at pictures. They are not interested in integrity at first sight as much as a big smile and a curvy figure. We know a brunette woman who put up her blonde friend's photo in her ad because her photo wasn't ready. Not one of the 50 men who responded noticed that the brunette was a blonde, even though her profile said she was a brunette. No one even asked her about it! The moral of the story: Men don't focus on what you write as long as they like your photo. One woman we know who posted an ad with a photo got 300 responses (some of which were high quality), versus 27 (less than desirable quality) responses for the same ad on another site without a photo.

We suggest you place one photo, not three or four (too desperate!), and make sure you are smiling in it. But no glamorous shots that look nothing like you, are 10 years old, or were taken before you gained 40 pounds. Honesty is the best policy here. There's nothing worse than a guy looking immediately disappointed on your first date. We have heard of men who actually told women that they didn't look as good as their photos. Do you really need to be insulted like that? We don't think so.

Just post a pretty (and recent!) headshot of you alone. A full-figure pose is also OK, as long as it is not come-hither-looking. And please, no photos of you with your breasts hanging out of your blouse. *The Rules* still apply online! If you show a lot of cleavage or pose like a *Playboy* model, you are going to attract sex addicts and "players." So the rule is: nothing too provocative.

We understand that some high-profile women may not want to post their photos for safety or privacy reasons, and we describe one such woman in *"Online Dating for Recognizable Personalities"* (page 198). But we have a hard time understanding why most women won't put up their pictures. We have heard of women with ex-boyfriends or ex-husbands on the same service, or successful businesswomen not wanting to post their photos lest their bosses, clients, coworkers, or even their kids and town know what they are doing. The truth usually is, they are embarrassed to be doing online dating at all.

One woman, a gynecologist in Chicago, told us, "I feel

funny putting up my photo. I do not want my patients to say, 'Look, there's my OB-GYN.'" Another woman, a vice president of sales for a network TV station, told us, "I would be mortified if my boss, my coworkers, sales reps, or the managers of affiliate stations around the country that I deal with saw my picture. You really think it's that important?"

We more or less told them, "Put up your photo anyway!" Don't worry, it's really not a big deal anymore and nothing to be embarrassed about. The point is, yes, if you want a great guy to answer your ad, you have to put up a photo. (Both the OB-GYN and TV executive complained that their ads without photos were getting them only mediocre or strange responses.)

Sometimes a woman will not post a photo at first, but as she gets more comfortable with online dating, she changes her mind. Some don't post a photo with their ad, but e-mail or send a man their photo afterward. Taking all this into account, every woman should do what she is most comfortable with at the time.

Rule 5

Wait 24 Hours to Respond

We know some women who respond to men's initial e-mails in nanoseconds—not even minutes, but nanoseconds. They stay on the computer all day as if they were on a fishing expedition, just waiting to catch a live one, hoping that a quick response will get a relationship going faster. This is a big mistake, it smacks of desperation, and it just doesn't work. When men you hardly know or recently met online hear from you too quickly or too constantly, they will think you have no life, even if your ad or profile states how busy and wonderful your life is!

You would think that we are talking about women who don't have much going on. On the contrary, these women are busy doctors, MBAs, and Wall Street analysts who are members of organizations and marathon runners with tons of friends who still manage to e-mail men back in five minutes. Unfortunately, they give men the impression that they are not very busy and much too eager.

So to give men the right impression—that you are a busy CUAO with hobbies and lots going on and hardly any time for chitchat—check your ad-related mail *only once a day*. Respond to any e-mails from potential dates met online or offline *24 hours after you receive them*. The most successful *Rules* girls say they put off reading men's e-mails until they are ready to answer them and, in general, limit their time on the computer, forcing themselves to do other activities such as sports and live singles events. There is nothing less effective than women e-mailing men back in nanoseconds.

If your job requires working on a computer all day, fine! That doesn't make it okay to e-mail and Instant Message men all day. Making men wait to hear from you is good for you—and for them. It creates desire, longing, and anticipation, which are the essence of *The Rules*. They make the chase that much sweeter, and they make every e-mail a man gets from you all the more precious. If a man hears from you too soon and too often, he will get bored before he even meets you, or soon thereafter.

We know a woman who simply could not abide by this *Rule*. She put up an ad with a photo and felt compelled to e-mail men back right away. Of course, these men poofed! Then her computer broke and she couldn't e-mail anyone for two weeks. You wouldn't believe how much excitement and interest this created. When her computer was finally fixed, she went online and found dozens of e-mails from men who'd responded to her ad and photo. Several of them had even sent repeated e-mails to her when she didn't respond to their first e-mails!

When she finally went online, she chose to e-mail back a dozen men, many of whom had sent repeated e-mails. She got back e-mails like, "Thought I would never hear from you, figured maybe you met some other lucky guy and left me in the dust. Don't want to lose this opportunity. Please give me your number. Are you free for dinner this Friday night?" This from a man who might have taken weeks to ask for her number had she e-mailed him back right away! When he thought she wasn't interested, it made him that much more interested and he suddenly wanted a date. Another man wrote, "Wow, I thought I got dumped! I wrote you three times—sorry about your computer. I was thinking maybe we could get together and I could give you any computer help you need."

Thanks to this lucky break, she ended up meeting all 12 guys because she took so long to e-mail them back, and is now engaged to one of them!

Don't wait to go to the Caribbean for a week or for your computer to be on the fritz to follow this rule! LOL! Just tell yourself or a *Rules*-minded friend that you will not reply before 24 hours later and then get busy with the rest of your life. This is a good character-building exercise—like working hard for a boss you don't particularly like or going to the gym when you don't feel like it. Just do it . . . or, rather, don't do it for 24 hours.

Remember, this 24-hour rule is just for the first few crucial months of courtship. As your relationship progresses and things go well with weekly dates and e-mails, you do not have to wait 24 hours to respond to a man's e-mails. An hour or two is reasonable, although waiting till the end of the day is even better. If you are home, take a walk. Make a phone call. Organize your closets. If you are at work, you can certainly find something to do. Call a client. Pay a bill. Write a memo. You can create some distance between you and that e-mail if you set your mind to it. Anything is better than e-mailing a man a minute later!

Rule 6

Don't Answer on Weekends or Holidays

You are a CUAO, confident and happy with a busy social schedule, so you have no time to answer men's e-mails on the weekends. After all, how sought-after and desirable will he think you are if you are hunched over a computer e-mailing him back at 10 P.M. on Saturday night?

On some services, men can see when you are reading their e-mail, and if you are doing so on Friday and Saturday nights or holiday times, you will not appear hard to get and busy. First impressions are everlasting, so give men the impression that you are busy with friends, family, parties, and even dates, not home in sweatpants online looking for love on match.com or americansingles.com.

Also refrain from responding to e-mails to your ad after midnight during the week or on Sundays before 5 P.M. It's too revealing for him to see you respond to him at 3 A.M. on a weeknight, and men should think you are having brunch or are at a concert or something else equally exciting on Sunday during the day. Wait until late Sunday afternoon when the weekend is nearly over. You should not be prowling online in chat rooms and dating services or e-mailing men back before then.

The only thing you should be doing online on the weekends is working, e-mailing friends, surfing the net, shopping—not singles-oriented things. Do not even log on to your chat room or dating service screen name at these times. This is going to be hard to do if you are impatient to meet someone and if you have a computer an arm's length away. You may have to call a *Rules*-minded girlfriend for support. You won't be alone. Some of the strictest *Rules* girls we know don't even look at their mail on weekends so as not to be tempted to e-mail back at these times.

You might notice that men e-mail women and answer ads at all hours, even Saturday nights. This is okay for men. Remember, dating isn't even-steven, and these *Rules* apply only to women. Don't ask why, just trust us, being on the computer on Friday or Saturday night is just not a CUAO thing to do! Do you really want men you barely know to know you are home with no plans on Saturday night? We don't think so. So don't e-mail men on weekends and let them all wonder where you are!

Rule 7

Write Light and Breezy E-mails

Online dating lends itself to soul-baring. You want to bare your heart and soul, you want to make an instant connection, you want to feel close to someone, you want to tell that person everything about your past and your present (especially at midnight after a bad blind date). You want that special someone to understand you and you him, you want to bond, and you want it all today, instantly!

Whether you were recently hurt or haven't been in a relationship for a while, you want immediate gratification and compensation for all the pain and heartache of recent years or even decades. But get a grip and tell yourself there is no shortcut to courtship, things take time, so you must not act impatiently or desperately. You are a CUAO, remember? You need to force yourself to refrain from saying anything too intense or negative that could scare a man away. Unfortunately, no matter what your heart says, you must hold back a bit for your own good.

Here are 14 *Rules* to help you be light and breezy in your e-mails:

1. Sometimes giving a man no answer is being light and breezy. If a man doesn't write you a sentence or two specific to your ad, but rather just sends you his profile through a "wink" or a "rose" (stock-response features that allow you to click on an ad and send your profile to the chosen ad), or if he sends a photo only, do not respond at all. It shows no effort, very little interest in you, merely a click of a button. Just delete it. He is just using online dating for fun, not to seriously meet someone. He's just cruising online.

2. If a man sends you an e-mail and he doesn't have a photo online, say "Would love to see a photo. Thanks." That's it, nothing else. Do not have a long conversation with this man no matter how interesting and long his e-mail to you was. If he refuses to send his photo, there is usually a reason. We are not being superficial here. When he does respond with a photo and you like it, do not write "Cute pic" or "Nice abs." Just say "Thanks for the photo" and answer his questions.

3. Don't tell a man you checked his profile, even if you did. Just write back in response to his e-mail, "You sound nice," and anything else you want to say. Do not write, "Read your ad, my brother is also an accountant, and he also played basketball in college. I love skiing and tennis too . . . We seem to have a lot in common." As a *Rules* girl, you are too busy to be memorizing men's ads, remember? Even though you did.

4. Do not look through his profile for conversation pieces. For example, do not notice that he is newly divorced

and say, "Sorry about your marriage . . . why did it end?" or see that he has two children and ask their ages. None of your business at this point. Save it for when you are dating awhile or when he brings it up. Also, don't ask questions about his work. It's an obvious ploy to find out how much money he makes and if he will be a good provider. Take a chance if you like him, don't worry about his income. Let him ask a few questions about you. Women tend to get into these long question-and-answer sessions with men online and it is a complete waste of time as most never even make it to date zero anyway.

5. Never e-mail a man a second time if he neglected to respond to your e-mail, even if you think that he is your future husband or soul mate. Never! E-mailing a man twice in a row is the antithesis of being light and breezy. He may be away on business or just busy, and you will come across as desperate, or he may just poof! If he does, just let him poof!

Don't think his or your computer is not working. On some systems, you can check sent mail to see if the e-mail has been read. Do not e-mail him, "Wasn't sure if you got my last e-mail . . ." He did! If he never e-mails you again, so be it, next! Just know that if you do e-mail him twice in a row and he responds, you will have made yourself the pursuer. He will know how much you like him, and the relationship will follow suit.

6. If you get any angry e-mails back, such as "I want more than three sentences from someone I would want to date, someone open and honest, no games," hit the delete button. More about that in *Rule 12: "Screen Out Mr. Wrong."* However, if a man writes back nicely and says "Tell me more

about yourself," you can tell him a hobby or two or favorite TV show or about your recent ski trip.

7. For the first three months, do not initiate e-mails; only respond to e-mails he sends you—and only if his e-mail merits a response to a question. Do not e-mail back if he sends you a joke or just says something like, "Did I tell you how adorable you are?" although if he sends these kinds of complimentary e-mails regularly you can wait for three to add up and e-mail back, "That is so sweet, thank you." Just wait 24 hours before you e-mail him back.

8. Don't be a downer. If you had a bad day, your job is on the line, money problems, health scare, and so on, do not weave it into your e-mail conversations as a way of bonding with this man. For example, don't say "Crazy week. 30 people were let go at work. I could be next. Mother just diagnosed with cancer. Last boyfriend was a jerk, hope you are different." This might be fine for your girlfriends, even a female acquaintance, but it is not the way to get close to a potential date. On the contrary, it will make the average man think "Nut case!" or "Who wants to hear her problems?" and he will never ask you out. Instead say, "Hi, got your e-mails . . . crazy busy with work . . . going to work out now and burn off some Italian food from last night . . . have a really great day . . ."

9. After three or four months, you can initiate one quick fun e-mail—such as a joke, or something that made you think of him, but nothing about sex, just a small inno-cent e-mail. For example, if he is a basketball fan and his favorite team lost the playoffs the night before, you can

e-mail him, "Hi, there. Hope you're doing well. Sorry about the Knicks. Maybe next year!"

10. Words never to use in your e-mails and things never to discuss in e-mails (even if he does):

soul mate
dream man
commitment
commitment-phobia
anything about sex
his or your long-term plans
ex-boyfriend
ex-husband
last relationship
marriage
connection
intimacy
or anything about game-playing (e.g., "I don't play games").

It all sounds good on paper, but you cannot write "soul mate" and think you will get one that way. A soul mate is someone who responds to your ad, doesn't give up e-mailing you, tries to get your number to get a date with you and is a loving and fun companion. Unfortunately, you cannot attract this by writing the word down any more than you can attract wealth by writing down the word "money." Be patient. More will be revealed. It takes time to figure out who your soul mate is. So beyond looking desperate, it is really a waste of time to write down "waiting for my soul mate" or anything like it.

11. Do not write anything about sex. If he does in the first few e-mails, that's probably all he wants, so delete/next! If he asks about a past relationship, just say "It didn't work out." Do not go into details, such as he wouldn't commit, he cheated on me. None of his business what happened.

12. Do not talk online about how you are doing with online dating. Sometimes a man will ask how long you have been dating online, if you like it, and if you've met any guys. He may be gathering information and really not be interested in you at all. The way to get out of this is to say you are new to online dating and haven't been paying attention, and don't answer his questions. If he says anything negative (such as all the women he's met are psychologically disturbed, shallow, and so on) and is just looking for a pity party about how hard it is to meet someone, say you like online dating and are having fun. Remember, *Rules* girls are CUAOs, happy, not negative. He may just want to vent; that's fine, but not with you. Dating online as in real life is not therapy, so don't go there. You want men to ask you out on dates, not have a debate.

13. Even if you are in a relationship, do not talk about anything too personal in an e-mail. You never know where it will end up. According to a *New York Post* article in December 2000, a 26-year-old British Public Relations executive sent her lawyer boyfriend an erotic e-mail using her work e-mail address. Big mistake! She bragged about a sexual act she had performed on him and how much she enjoyed it. He forwarded her e-mail to six of his lawyer friends at the firm with the note, "Now that's a nice compliment from a lass, isn't it?" His coworkers passed it on to

their friends. Within 24 hours, the salacious correspondence was copied, forwarded, and sent to millions of people all over the globe, including Australia and Japan. The couple was so inundated by the tabloids that they went into hiding. According to the *Post*, "The couple's excruciating story is a cautionary tale about how fast your most personal e-mail can be duplicated." In other words, don't be a laughing stock. Don't talk about your sex life online. If you are going to talk about it at all, save it for the date.

14.   Other topics not to talk about in e-mails are your "needs." Talk about scaring men away! We know of one woman who met a man in a chat room, she'd spoken to him first, and she'd been the one who kept the relationship going with lots of e-mails. After two dates and a month of fast and furious e-mails back and forth, she wrote the following e-mail to him:

> *Dear Jeff,*
>
> *You are giving me mixed messages and I have to say I don't like it one bit. On the one hand, you show a lot of interest in your e-mails and Instant Messages but then you rarely follow up with calls and dates. Two dates in a month is not exactly my idea of intimacy. I know you are getting over a divorce and a bad rebound relationship, but your past (and mine) doesn't have to be our future. We can start fresh if you will only give us a chance. I am not looking for the moon, I just want to spend Saturday nights with a special someone. You? Is that too much to ask? The next dinner is on me.*
>
> *Lots of kisses,*
> *Lori*

A *Rules* Girl only loves those who love her. This woman is obviously not doing *The Rules* and her e-mail shows that she's under the erroneous impression that she can argue a man into wanting to spend time with her. He either does or he doesn't.

Here is Jeff's e-mail back to her four days later (he was in no rush to respond):

> *Dear Lori:*
>
> *I have enjoyed the time we have spent together but as I told you and you don't seem to remember or don't want to remember, I am not interested in a full-time relationship with anyone right now including you. I just can't commit to every Saturday night right now. For one thing, I want to spend more time with my son and I am just getting out of a six-month relationship. I need a break, no hassle, no demands. This in no way diminishes my feelings for you. I think you are special, but I cannot give you what you want. Work is hectic, ex-wife is a pain, will have to take a rain check on dinner.*
>
> > *Be well,*
> > *Jeff*

Jeff basically gave her the kiss-off, but he tried to be kind about it. Unfortunately, Lori may take some of what he said—such as "you are special"—as a reason to keep e-mailing him and waiting for dates. The point is that stating her "needs" proved "needy"—and needless. She should have just told or e-mailed her friends about her frustrations with Jeff. Jeff now knows exactly how she feels and this has made him back off even more.

So basically keep your e-mails light, two to three sentences—"Work is crazy. Off to a meeting. Gotta go"—and save the discussions for your dates. No smiley faces. No horizons. No cutesy coffee cups. And no "friendship" greetings. All that shows too much interest and effort. Remember, you are a CUAO—men are calling and e-mailing you for dates day and night. You don't have a minute to send an online morning bouquet!

Rule 8

Block Yourself from Instant Messages

The Internet is breeding a new kind of privacy invasion. First there was the answering machine. Before this handy device was around, you never knew if a guy called or not, unless you had a roommate, or lived at home and your mother answered the phone. With the answering machine, girls started reporting back to us scenes such as the following: "I had a fight with my boyfriend and there were like six hang-up messages on my machine—it must have been him!" Thus a new kind of tracking system was born.

Next came the dial *69 phone feature that allows you to trace the last incoming call you've received. If a boyfriend wanted to check up on you, he could call and hang up on you just to see if you were home, but with *69, that anonymity is gone—you can dial *69 to retrieve the last phone number dialed, and see if your boyfriend was checking up on you!

Well, now the Internet is the new tracking system, causing

privacy issues and making it difficult for *Rules* girls to be mysterious. It used to be if you sat home on a Friday or Saturday night and ordered in a pizza or Chinese food, no one knew except your close girlfriends and the delivery guy. Now, with the Internet, everyone is potentially an open book.

For example, the largest Internet provider, America Online, has a feature called a "Buddy List"—an AOL feature designed to let a user know if people whose e-mail addresses he's placed on his Buddy List are online or not. There's also a feature on some online dating services that lets everyone logged into the site know if and when you've logged into the dating service. So if your e-mail address is on someone's AOL Buddy List, or if you are on a provider with a similar service, or if you've logged into an online dating service with a feature that shows you've logged in, others will know you're online and then can Instant Message you.

Without knowing *The Rules* for online dating, you would probably not "block" yourself (blocking is a feature that allows you to be on the computer without anyone knowing, even if you're on someone's Buddy List; also, some online dating services offer you a type of blocking feature that allows you to remain "invisible" when logged into that service). Instead, you might remain visible and available to any man who could then Instant Message you and draw you into an IM conversation, and you could end up potentially wasting one or two hours chatting with a guy who may just be bored or lonely. And even if he doesn't e-mail or IM you, he knows you're at home and at the computer! Do you want everyone to know that?

We suggest a *Rules*-y approach to this invasion of privacy: Block yourself so he does not know when you are online. If a blocking option is available on the online dating service you subscribe to, choose that option. If you meet him in a chat room or he contacts you when you're logged onto a dating service, you can have an initial Instant Message (or chat) with him—but only if *he* IMs you first or initiates the chat. After you leave the chat room or log off the dating service, he will have to e-mail you.

It's great that you have this opportunity to meet people with similar interests in a chat room, but now he needs to pursue you in a more definite way. This will prevent the relationship, if there is one, from becoming too casual and last-minute. If you cannot block yourself, simply cancel or delete the Instant Messages you receive. When you delete his IMs, he will have to use the more formal, regular e-mail to contact you, which takes more time and thought on his part than an Instant Message. Most men are used to Instant Messaging and being Instant Messaged by non-*Rules* girls, talking for hours and giving it no more thought than lunch, so it may take them a while to realize you are different and e-mail you.

You may be wondering why we are so against Instant Messaging. Simply put, it is too casual and spontaneous in a bad way. It is as if a man came knocking on your door without any notice, found you at home, and walked right in. It's like a guy running into you on the street and getting to chat with you on the corner. How hard is that? If you let yourself be so available, you will cease to be a challenge and then men will not have to work hard to see you (for example, ask you out by Wednesday for Saturday). Everything will come too easy for them, it will throw the relationship off balance, and they will probably get bored and move on to someone else. Whether online or in person, you must give men the impression that the only way they can speak to you or see you is by booking time with you in advance.

Here is a typical scenario. Robin (GreatCatch) posted an ad and Eric (OneForYou44) liked it; he responded to it with "You're very pretty. Hope we can chat sometime. I put you on my Buddy List."

She e-mailed him back, "Sure!" That night when she was online, she got an Instant Message from him and the following dialogue ensued:

OneForYou44: *Hi! I'm Eric. Remember me?*

GreatCatch29: *Sure. Hi there, I'm Robin.*

OneForYou44: *So what are you up to?*

GreatCatch29: *Just catching up on some paperwork.*

OneForYou44: *Sorry, am I interrupting?*

GreatCatch29: *No, I was just finishing up.*

OneForYou44: *So what do you do for a living? Sorry, I can't remember.*

GreatCatch29: *I'm a headhunter.*

OneForYou44: *Cool. Can you find me a job? I haven't been happy with my job for six months.*

GreatCatch29: *What do you do?*

OneForYou44: *Accountant, CPA.*

GreatCatch29: *E-mail me your resume. I'll see.*

OneForYou44: *OK. So what did you do today?*

GreatCatch29: *I called clients to get leads and organized files.*

OneForYou44: *I can relate to that, LOL! So have you met anyone online?*

GreatCatch29: *A few guys.*

OneForYou44: *Anyone good?*

GreatCatch29: *No. What about you?*

OneForYou44: *A couple of girls. I think most women are just interested in looks and money. Am I right?*

GreatCatch29: *I'm not like that.*

OneForYou44: *Good. So what's your story? Have you ever been married?*

GreatCatch29: *Engaged once.*

OneForYou44: *What happened?*

GreatCatch29: *He got cold feet. What about you?*

OneForYou44: *Divorced twice, one kid.*

GreatCatch29: *Boy or girl? How old?*

This went on for two hours. They Instant Messaged each other about his kids, their backgrounds, their exes, their jobs, blind dates, and so on, and at the end he gave her his number and said "Call me sometime" but never asked her out.

Another reason not to accept Instant Messages is that it often degenerates into sex and sleaze. Duh, what else do you think is on men's minds, especially after midnight?

Here is an Instant Message scenario that exemplifies this. Harvey noticed Lisa's ad on a dating service and thought she was cute.

CoolGuy39: *Liked your ad and thought I would say hi. I'm Harvey. Am I interrupting anything?*

HotBabe32: *I'm Lisa. No, just hanging out.*

CoolGuy39: *I noticed you said you work at a law firm. What do you do?*

HotBabe32: *I'm a paralegal. What about you?*

CoolGuy39: *I'm a lawyer, big coincidence. So let's cut to the chase. What are you wearing?*

HotBabe32: *A man's T-shirt.*

CoolGuy39: *Is there a man there too or just the T-shirt? LOL.*

HotBabe32: *Just the T-shirt.*

CoolGuy39: Who gave it to you? An old boyfriend?

HotBabe32: Yes, I kept it when we broke up. LOL.

CoolGuy39: Anything under the T-shirt?

HotBabe32: Maybe . . . maybe not.

CoolGuy39: Wow! I'm getting excited just thinking about it. Maybe I'll come over and see for myself. Where do you live?

HotBabe32: It's after midnight! I'm going to bed soon.

CoolGuy39: I'll tuck you in. Seriously, I'm already dressed and out the door. What's your address?

HotBabe32: I'm not telling you where I live, but I'll meet you at an all-night diner in the neighborhood for coffee.

CoolGuy39: OK, can't wait.

So in about ten minutes this guy has a coffee date with a woman he Instant Messaged once, and if he gets really lucky he may end up in her apartment after this particular date zero. This is faster than any call-girl service—and cheaper!

Sometimes it takes a longer Instant Message exchange or several Instant Message sessions to get to this point. They may chat for an hour or two or even for a couple of weeks about this, that, and the other thing before they actually meet, but invariably it ends with "What are you wearing?" or "Have you ever considered a threesome?"

So if you want a man to respect you and not treat you like a last-minute girl, don't accept Instant Messages. Let him think you are busy or don't know how to Instant Message. It really doesn't matter what he thinks as long as he e-mails you and eventually asks you out. And then on the date you can talk about work and anything else you want.

Rule 9

Rules for Chat Rooms

Chat rooms are like bars. Imagine men and women sitting around on bar stools or mingling and making jokes with drinks in their hands. Think *Sex and the City* meets *Cheers*. The only difference is no one knows what anyone else looks like—it's like one big blind date. The only things people have to go on are each other's screen names.

So how exactly do you do *The Rules* in a chat room?

Simple. You go in quietly. You are not the loud-mouthed one who barges in asking "So what's up?" When you do speak up, you don't say anything to anyone in particular, and you certainly don't single out any man, even if his screen name is NiceGuy35. For example, you do not say "Hi, NiceGuy, how nice are you? LOL."

You talk to the group as a whole, the stars, the moon, the universe, if you will, anyone but him.

Chat rooms usually have a topic for discussion, and topics can range from "singles" to "politics" to "sports." When you go into a chat room, a conversation will be in progress. Don't interrupt, go with whatever the conversation is. You don't start a new conversation, you don't argue with anyone or put anyone down. You are sober in the chat room, not drunk or silly.

You do not talk about sex or anything compromising. The *Rule* is: If you wouldn't say it in a bar, don't say it in a chat room. You would not yell out loud about your sex life or your last relationship in a bar. You talk about work, politics, or sports. Ditto for chat rooms.

When a man Instant Messages you, you pause before you push "reply." Specifically, we suggest you count to 20 when responding to an Instant Message with a new man. And if no man Instant Messages you, you eventually log off. That's it.

Most women are not doing *The Rules* in chat rooms. They are being unusually aggressive both in chat rooms and Instant Message sessions that follow, maybe because it is all so anonymous. For example, several men we spoke to complained that women will ask a million questions in rapid-fire succession: "How old are you?" "What do you do?" "How's the dating going?" "Are you serious or just wasting my time?" If the men don't answer right away, the women get annoyed and even nasty and say things like, "Where are you?" or "You're busy chatting with someone else, aren't you?" It is a big turn-off, they say, because they go into chat rooms to relax, have some fun conversation at a leisurely pace, meet new people, not get interrogated.

Here is a typical scenario. LookinForLuv32 is in a chat room for an hour when MrFixIt41 comes in:

MrFixIt41 writes in the room: *Anyone pretty and available in here?*

LookinForLuv32 writes in the room: *I am!*

Then she immediately Instant Messages him first.

LookinForLuv32: *Hi!*

MrFixIt41: *A.S.L. [Age, Sex, Location]*

LookinForLuv32: *32, female, from Miami. My name is Mindy. What's yours?*

MrFixIt41: *Mark. So what's up?*

LookinForLuv32: *Just hanging out. So what do you fix?*

MrFixIt41: *Broken hearts! LOL! No, I'm a contractor, I renovate homes.*

LookinForLuv32: *Cool! I'm redoing my kitchen, lots of work, but I guess you know that.*

MrFixIt41: *If you need any help, let me know. I'm handy and good-looking too. Divorced, two kids.*

She e-mails him her photo.

MrFixIt41: *You're very hot. So what's your story?*

LookinForLuv32: *Divorced, no kids, meeting lots of men here, but looking for that special someone. Are you really divorced or just separated? What happened?*

MrFixIt41: *Signing divorce papers soon. Nothing happened. That's the problem. No sex. I bet you're a real sex kitten.*

LookinForLuv32: *You're right about that. No one's ever complained. Send me your photo. Where do you live?*

MFixIt41: *Don't have a photo yet. But you won't be disappointed. I've been told I look like Andy Garcia. I'm in Boca, not far from you.*

LookinForLuv32: *I love Andy Garcia! Why don't you stop by this Saturday and look at my kitchen? Make a house call LOL! I'm free the whole weekend.*

MrFixIt41: *I have the kids this weekend, maybe another time. So have you met anyone good through this?*

LookinForLuv32: *Dated a guy for six months who was separated, but he went back to his wife, sleeps in her bed every night now. Broke my heart. I said never again. Must be divorced or nothing doing. I have so much to offer, won't settle with just any guy. I want a guy who gives 100 percent, nothing less. Do you have a lot to give, I mean emotionally?*

MrFixIt41: *If we click, I promise you, you'll get everything, my heart and soul. What went wrong with your marriage?*

LookinForLuv32: *He was cheating on me and like a fool I kept giving him chances, then I cheated on him with his best friend just to get even and he found out and just had a fit and he ended up divorcing me. He married his secretary, the one he was screwing around with. We don't speak. But enough about him. . . . When can I see you? I'm in sales, so I make my own hours.*

MrFixIt41 doesn't answer for a few minutes.

LookinForLuv32: *Are you still there? Talking to somebody else?*

MrFixIt41: *Calm down, just busy with work. Plumber on the phone. Work is really crazy right now and I have my kids for the next two weekends. Ex is going on vacation with new boyfriend . . . so will get back to you.*

LookinForLuv32: *Don't forget me . . . I'm easy to love. Not like your ex. LOL!*

MrFixIt41: *Forget you? Not a chance. I'm getting excited just thinking about you. . . . But I gotta go . . . I have a big deadline on a house. Talk soon.*

LookinForLuv32: *OK, bye, e-mail me soon!*

If you think this is a steamy scene out of *Sex and the City* and would never happen in real life, you're wrong. This kind of exchange goes on all day long in chat rooms across the Internet.

Notice that breaking one *Rule* leads to breaking another and another. First broken *Rule:* LookingforLuv32 spoke to MrFix-It41 first by answering his question ("Anyone pretty and available?") which was directed to the whole room, not her. That was her first mistake. She should have continued to write in the room about general stuff ("Did anyone watch *ER* last night?") until he singled her out because he liked her screen name or liked what she had to say. And if he didn't, oh well. Then she broke another rule by Instant Messaging him, then she responded to "A.S.L.," which a *Rules* girl would never do. "A.S.L." does not even merit a response. It shows absolutely no effort and no interest, like drinking in a bar. Even in a chat room, a man should be trying to charm you by saying things like "Love your screen name" or "You sound interesting, what do you look like?" "A.S.L." is just collecting data, like an accountant.

Then she broke another *Rule* by telling him her whole life story and suggesting they meet. She also started interrogating him when he didn't respond right away at one point. In every way, she is the aggressor in the IM exchange. Worst of all, she does not end the Instant Message first. She should have been the one to say, "Work is busy. I have to call back three customers," and logged off first.

Even if she is unemployed, she should say, "Oops, my toast is burning . . ." and end the Instant Message first. Yes, you can be funny, if necessary, but don't let a man log off first. The chat-room relationship you read about above is nothing you would want, even if you are as desperate as LookingforLuv32 apparently is. (And by the way, her screen name is all wrong. See

Rule 2.) So even if MrFixIt41 does e-mail her again and they even date for a while, it will never be anything. He may visit her for quick sex and forget about her five minutes later because she initiated the relationship and it was all sex talk and all too easy.

Contrast this to a *Rules* girl (JenAniston-ish34) who went into a local singles chat room. TallDarkHandsome39 Instant Messaged her right away.

TallDarkHandsome39: *Do you really look like Jennifer Aniston? I love* Friends! *Do you have a pic?*

JenAniston-ish34: *My friends tell me so. I definitely have her hair. I have an ad up on love@aol.*

TallDarkHandsome39: *I just checked your ad. Wow! So what is a pretty girl like you doing in here?*

JenAniston-ish34: *Just thought it might be fun to meet new people.*

TallDarkHandsome39: *Have you met anyone?*

JenAniston-ish34: *This is my first time . . . just came in 10 minutes ago.*

TallDarkHandsome39: *You really are beautiful!*

JenAniston-ish34: *You are very sweet!*

TallDarkHandsome39: *Maybe we could meet for a drink or dinner.*

Jen waits and counts to 20 (so she seems like she's thinking about it and not desperate).

JenAniston-ish34: *That sounds nice.*

TallDarkHandsome39: *Can I get your phone number?*

Jen waits and counts to 20.

JenAniston-ish34: *Sure, my cell is 555-3322. But I have to go now, my boss just walked in. Bye!*

TallDarkHandsome39: *Okay. I'll call you.*

If you want a role model to follow, JenAniston-ish34 is it. Her screen name is intriguing enough to make men Instant Message her, she does not volunteer her photo or her phone number, and she ends the Instant Message first.

By the way, she and TallDarkHandsome39 dated for six months. He was smitten and, although she liked him a lot, he was not the love of her life. She eventually met her husband (GreatGuy34) in the same local singles chat room a year later.

Rule 10

Don't Volunteer Your Phone Number First

One of the frustrations of online dating is that most men don't necessarily come right out and say, "What is your telephone number?" in their first few e-mails or as quickly as you would like them to. The biggest online complaint we hear from women goes something like this: "He's asked me about my job, my dog, my hair color, my hobbies. He's even alluded to getting together. When is he going to ask me for my phone number?"

In real life, the average man would ask for your number within the first meeting, sometimes within the first 20 minutes. Otherwise, he'd have no way of getting in touch with you. In the online world, a man may even suggest getting together, saying things like, "We should really go out sometime," which makes you think it's OK to volunteer your number first. It's not.

Here is a typical scenario.

A man's first e-mail may say, "Tell me more about yourself . . ." In the second e-mail he may tell you more about himself and ask you questions like "Have you been doing online dating a long time? Met anyone?"

His third e-mail may be about what he is looking for in a woman or what he liked about your ad, or more about your day, but still nothing about your telephone number, as if he had all the time in the world. At this point you want to scream, "Ask me for my number already!" but you're trying to be a *Rules* girl so you can't. But you are getting increasingly impatient with MrNiceGuy52, so you decide to take matters into your own hands and volunteer your number to get things going.

This is a big mistake which many online women make. He must specifically ask you, "Can I have your telephone number?" or, at the very least, he should give you his phone number, at which point you can then reciprocate by e-mailing him your phone number. But don't call him! There are two kinds of men who give you their phone number online, rather than come right out and ask you for yours. There is the "player": he just wants 50 women to call him. And then there's the nice guy who feels that you may be more comfortable calling him, a stranger, rather than having him call you. He's just being polite. The only way to really tell the difference between the two is to e-mail him your phone number and see if he calls. But never call him first.

Also, don't e-mail your phone number to a man who says "Let's chat sometime," even if he suggests you get together with a bookmark invitation like "We should really go out sometime." (A bookmark is when a man asks you out with no definite date.) This does not warrant your e-mailing him your number. Women tend to e-mail all their phone numbers (home, work, cell) just because a guy says these things. Do not be aggressive and rush things. Wait until he asks for your number, and then give him only one number—preferably, a cell phone number.

So the rule is: If a man writes "Call me sometime" and gives you his number, do not call him. In addition, don't e-mail him back and say "I don't call men" or "You have to call me" or anything like that, since that's tipping your hand. Simply wait 24 hours, then e-mail him back, "Thanks for your number, here's mine as well, 555-6263" and wait for him to call you. We know that for safety reasons, some women prefer to call men than be called. These women should give a cell number. Yes, you should have a cell phone to do online dating!

Most women do not know this. For example, Megan, 32, was doing online dating and truly enjoying this new way of meeting men. She lived in a suburb populated by families and sometimes felt like the only single girl in town! Like everyone else, when she first heard about online dating, she was a little apprehensive, thinking it might be unsafe, but after joining a *Rules* support group she decided to try it. She put up an ad with a photo and was thrilled to have men from the next city e-mailing her, men she would normally never meet.

Megan wrote to us saying that she liked online dating, but was having trouble getting some of these guys to ask for her phone number. She wanted to know if she was doing anything wrong, as some seemed content to just e-mail her. She wanted to know if it would be okay to casually write her number in an e-mail; after all, they'd shown initial interest by answering her ad. We told her no and explained that it was the same as writing your phone number down in a bar on the back of a matchbook and giving it to a man who approached you but hadn't asked for your number.

Megan said she still wondered why some men were content

to just chat forever while others asked for her number after two or three e-mails. We explained that some men are online to get pen pals, not meet women, so there was no use in volunteering her number.

As we told Megan and other women in our consultations, volunteering your phone number before a man asks for it is forward, especially online, and he will know it is an obvious ploy to make a premature connection. Don't try to make something happen that isn't supposed to happen online (or in real life). Remember at all times, you are a CUAO. Any man would be lucky to have your number and call you! You are not in a rush, your life doesn't depend on this one man, and there are other fish in the sea!

If He Doesn't Ask You Out within Four E-mails, Delete/Next!

Ideally, you want a man to ask you out as soon as possible to move the relationship from the computer to a date. But you cannot tell him to do this or even hint it. On the other hand, you should not wait forever. We think four e-mails is enough. If, by his fourth e-mail, a man hasn't suggested meeting, don't e-mail him again. He may just need a "push" to ask you out—and by that, we don't mean you should suggest to him that he ask you out. We mean you should simply drop out: Stop e-mailing him!

Most women hang in there way too long, sometimes as long as six months, waiting and hoping for a man to ask them out. We've heard of men who are still talking about politics, workout routines, and past relationships in their tenth e-mail. For whatever reason, they can't get around to saying "Let's meet" and following through with it.

Ed (Entrepreneur40) is a perfect example. He answered

Suzanne's ad (SassyGirl39) and she was thrilled, as he was not only handsome but seemed worldly as well. Never married and very particular, Ed thought Suzanne was attractive, but he was in no rush to ask her out. He asked her lots of questions, everything from the weather to hobbies and vacation spots. Suzanne was only too happy to answer every single one, all the time wondering if he was ever going to ask her out! She didn't realize that by responding to him, she was preventing herself from getting a date.

Here are their e-mail exchanges over a period of three weeks:

FIRST E-MAIL:

Entrepreneur40: *When I saw your ad, I thought, very pretty. I would have answered it sooner, but I had a top priority project to do. I'm an environmental engineer by day and an entrepreneur on the side, kind of a workaholic. Now that that's done, I can concentrate on you. I have to say you look familiar. Where are you from?*

SassyGirl39: *I grew up in Buffalo, New York. I live in New Jersey now.*

SECOND E-MAIL:

Entrepreneur40: *You're kidding. I went to college in Buffalo. SUNY-Buffalo. I skied there a hundred times. Worst snow storms I ever saw in my life. Do you like to ski?*

SassyGirl39: *I know, growing up I never took off my ski jacket and snow boots. I love to ski too. I have a ski share in Pennsylvania.*

THIRD E-MAIL:

Entrepreneur40: *I just got back from skiing in Italy, nothing like it. It was half business/half pleasure, two weeks. I could live there in a heartbeat. Have you been to Europe? Do you like to travel?*

SassyGirl39: *I lived in England on a semester abroad 20 years ago and France for work two years ago. I work in public relations for Hermes, the scarf company. But I've never been to Italy. Sounds wonderful, maybe someday. I love pasta, that's for sure.*

FOURTH E-MAIL:

Entrepreneur40: *Me too. Fettucine Alfredo is my favorite. I know this great Italian restaurant we can go to sometime. What do you like to do for fun? I'm a gambling man myself. I go to Atlantic City five times a year. Won $500 last time, but lost $1,200 the time before that, but hey, it's a blast. I stay at lavish penthouse suites, catch a few shows, spend some play money. Have you ever been to Las Vegas? Or maybe you're an Atlantic City girl?*

SassyGirl39: *I've been to Atlantic City twice, saw Earth, Wind and Fire once and a comedian another time, I forget his name, maybe Don Rickles, lost $25 in the slot machine both times, walked on the boardwalk. I don't play cards. It was fun.*

This is the e-mail Suzanne should never have sent, the point at which she should have just stopped corresponding with Ed. After four e-mails, it's time for a man to ask you out. If he wants to find out what you like to do for fun, or about your career and family, then he should ask you face-to-face on a date.

Think of four e-mails back and forth between you and a man you've met online as the equivalent of a half an hour talking to a guy you've met in a bar or a party. If, after 30 minutes, he hasn't asked for your number, you have to look at your watch and say, "Wow, I really have to get going," or "My ride is leaving, I have to go," in hopes that that will prompt him to ask for your number or risk never seeing you again. If you hang out all night waiting for him to ask for your number, you won't be a challenge and he may never ask.

All Ed really needed was a *Rules*-y girl who would not give him hours of time, or, in the online world, someone who would not be content chatting so easily and indefinitely. Men think when you chat with them endlessly that you will chat with anyone endlessly and that you're probably not very discriminating. A man should have to work hard on some level to get all this information out of you. He should at least take you out on a date!

Suzanne was too available online and not a challenge, so Ed lost interest. Although he did allude to taking her out for dinner, it was more of a "bookmark," with no definite date. He did not follow up by asking her for her number. Instead, he changed the subject and asked even more questions.

Had Suzanne stopped e-mailing him, he might have thought, "She won't e-mail me back. I guess I'll have to make specific plans with her." Allowing the e-mail correspondence to go beyond four e-mails ensured that Ed would get bored and Suzanne would get frustrated.

Here are the remaining e-mails between them:

FIFTH E-MAIL:

Entrepreneur40: *I'm going to Vegas tomorrow. I have an engineering convention there, five days, all expenses paid. Can't wait. Need some R&R, this project was grueling. PR sounds fun. What exactly do you do?*

SassyGirl39: *I try to get Hermes mentioned in magazines and newspapers, deal with any disgruntled customers, you know, celebrities and royalty and such. I send actresses and VIPs free samples hoping they will wear them in their next movie, that kind of thing. Can't complain. I have like 100 Hermes scarves in my closet.*

SIXTH E-MAIL:

Entrepreneur40: *Sounds neat. Do you like sports? I'm a sports fanatic. Basketball, baseball, football, I watch sports all the time. ESPN is my middle name. I also go to the gym, run three miles a day.*

SassyGirl39: *Wow! Very impressive. I ski, play tennis, and take kick-boxing classes at the gym. I have two brothers so I know all about sports.*

SEVENTH E-MAIL:

Entrepreneur40: *Are you close? I'm an only child. Wish I had siblings, but my father died when I was three. So it was just me and my mother. She never remarried, she just couldn't get over my father's death. He was killed in a car accident on his way home from work. There were a dozen roses on the seat next to him that he was going to give her that night. They were so in love.*

SassyGirl39: *Sorry about your father. Must have been hard growing up without one. My dad died last year at the age of 69.*

EIGHTH E-MAIL:

Entrepreneur40: *Sorry. So, I guess I should ask the obvious question. Why is a pretty girl like you never married?*

SassyGirl39: *Good question . . . I guess I haven't met the right one. What about you?*

NINTH E-MAIL:

Entrepreneur40: *Obsessed with work my whole life, I support my mother, we're very close, and I just never made dating a priority, until now. Determined to change all that. Want to get married and have kids, more than one!*

SassyGirl39: *Sounds good. I always wanted to have two, a boy and a girl.*

TENTH E-MAIL:

Entrepreneur40: *Well, it's late and I have to pack for Vegas. Have a 8 A.M. flight and then when I get back I have to put my mother in a nursing home. She's 80 and getting worse and worse. I'll be in touch.*

SassyGirl39: *Hope you have a fun trip and good luck with your mom. Bye!*

Ed e-mailed her a week later about his trip to Vegas (he won $700 at blackjack), and about his mother's declining health, but he still didn't ask for Suzanne's number. She e-mailed him back, and then he poofed! She never heard from him again.

We are not surprised. When a man takes more than four e-mails to ask you out, it is not a good sign. Sometimes he may need a push—the one girl who is too busy to e-mail him back forever. That is the one he will pursue.

Unfortunately, most women continue e-mailing men after four exchanges, often wasting weeks or months with these men. *Rules* girls don't; they set limits. Of course, we don't tell men what these limits are, we just stop e-mailing them back after four exchanges. We do not say, "We've been chatting for a while, do you want to meet or are you just going to waste my time?" or even the more subtle but equally manipulative, "I'm not big on e-mailing, I'm better in person," in hopes that he will ask you out, or even "My nails break when I type . . ." Hint, hint!

As we've said before, breaking one *Rule* leads to breaking another. Women who continue to chat past the fourth e-mail usually end up volunteering their phone number, in the hope that it will lead to a date. They usually end up frustrated by these men anyway. These men don't call regularly, they ask them out at the last minute, or they find trivial excuses to break up—one man broke up with a woman because they couldn't agree on what movie to see on their third date, which led to a fight. In plain English, they break up with you because they weren't that interested to begin with.

So if you keep writing a man back after he hasn't asked to meet by his fourth e-mail, you are asking for trouble down the road. He may get to know you so well online that his desire to meet you evaporates (poof!). In the online world, as in real life, familiarity breeds contempt. Just cut your losses, delete/next! and move on. Of course, if after you stop e-mailing him, he e-mails you that he wants to meet you and actually asks you out, you can go out with him. Sometimes a man won't get serious unless he realizes that you have moved on!

Rule 12

Screen Out Mr. Wrong

In *The Rules II,* we told you to watch for bad behavior (anger, sarcasm, excessive drinking, and so on) on the first few dates. In the online world, the screening process should start with his first e-mail to you. You must screen for the following:

form letters
e-mails from men without photos
e-mails from men without words
players
sex addicts
time-wasters
married men looking for a little action on the side.

We address time-wasters and married men in *Rules 13* and *21,* respectively.

When you first put your ad online, you feel as though you

won the lottery. You turn on your computer to find 50 to 100 responses blinking at you, just begging to be opened. You gleefully open each one as if you were about to bite into a Godiva chocolate. "Yummy," you think, "and I don't even have to leave the house!"

But just as bingeing on candy can result in a sugar hangover, expecting too much from these e-mails will surely lead to disappointment. Sadly, you realize that only 25 of those 100 responses have potential. As the saying goes, if it seems too good to be true, it probably is.

Unlike at a party where the average guy may ask one or two women to dance in an evening, in cyberspace, a man can easily e-mail 25 women at once. Each woman thinks his e-mail to her is special and precious, not realizing that it is a mass mailing that is virtually meaningless unless he plans to meet her. After all, it takes some effort to walk over to a woman at a party and strike up a conversation, whereas it takes almost no effort to push a button and send a form letter or "wink." So don't put your heart and soul into it or start planning the wedding based on any first e-mails. *Rules* girls have been known to say, "Mr. E-mail Man doesn't exist until you see the whites of his eyes!"

So if you don't want to get your hopes up high or waste a lot of time e-mailing virtual men or meeting crazy men, you must screen with a vengeance. Here are 10 screening tips:

1. Ask for a photo right away. Any man who sends an e-mail without a photo or posts an ad without one either isn't serious about meeting someone, has a girlfriend, is using online dating as a game like Pac-Man, or is hiding something. When a woman doesn't post or send a photo, it is often for safety reasons. But we have found that when a

man doesn't, it is usually not for the same reason. Your response should be "Thanks for your e-mail, but I'd love to see a photo." If he still doesn't send one, delete/next! Do not be persuaded by men who beg you to give them a chance without a photo, even if they use celebrity descriptions.

Here is one such e-mail that deserves a delete/next!:

> I'd love to send you a picture . . . alas, though, I don't have one scanned. I can promise, guarantee, and am so certain that you will find me incredibly sexy, just trust me a tiny bit. Please. I could describe myself . . . I'm 6', 190 pounds. Jet black hair, medium length. Big, soft, deep brown eyes. Nice hands. Long legs. Lean, muscular frame. Imagine George Clooney.

Next! Men who are unwilling to send a photo without giving you a really good reason—for example, "I am a surgeon and president of my hospital and for privacy purposes cannot send my photo, but I am for real. I will call you tonight at 9:00 if you give me your number"—should be delete/next-ed! In some cases, even these men with good excuses are not presidents of hospitals; they usually just have girlfriends or may even be married.

2. Be wary of men with too many photos. If he e-mails you and you check his ad and there are six photos—for example, him alone, him and his nephew, him and his dog, him at the beach, him on a boat, and the fish he caught on the boat, or he sends you all these when you exchange photos—watch out! He may be much too into this and enjoying cyberspace too much to have a real relationship, or he could be a big time-waster. The average guy looking for a

relationship would post one photo, or maybe two, or have one photo available to send, period.

3. No words, no response. As we stated earlier, men who simply send you a "wink," a "rose," or write "you're hot," should not get a response. They are either lazy, just looking for fun, or have a girlfriend. They will usually poof! so delete/next! You want a man who reads your ad and writes you something, however short, and specific to you.

4. Don't get excited by form letters. It is easy to spot a form letter: It is long, romantic, and exciting, but it says nothing about you or your ad. It will be all about him and his hopes and dreams. How else can he send the same thing to everyone? You can choose to delete form letters or you can respond with "You sound nice" but realize that he sent the same note to 100 other women.

So don't expect much even if his form letter contains everything you want to hear, such as "I want to share a gentle August breeze and moonlit sky over a dinner table on a quiet Venice canal, as I look into your eyes and we toast at midnight to the beginning of something special" that literally sends goose bumps up your spine (especially after your last three unromantic ex-boyfriends) and makes you want to call a travel agent immediately to book that Venice vacation with this virtual stranger. He may very well poof! after that one e-mail.

A man who really wants to meet someone and have a relationship would read your ad and write a note specific to you. The best e-mails come from men who pick up on something you wrote, for example, "You like to watch the

Food Network and cook up recipes too? I have to meet you. What is your number?"

5. Watch for "player" screen names. Screen names say a lot about a man. Men with screen names such as PlayTime2002, SensualOne, or TarzanYourMan are probably players. You want to hear from men with screen names like James245 or NiceGuy629, who appear to be truly looking to meet women.

6. Don't argue with angry men. Sadly, we have found that some men take out their anger at women in general (or at their last five ex-girlfriends) online. They will get angry if a woman doesn't write back right away, or if she doesn't write enough, or if she refuses to meet for dinner. Some *Rules* girls we know who wrote short responses or said they preferred to meet for drinks (a short date, only one to two hours) as opposed to meeting for dinner (three or four hours) received such angry e-mails from men.

One wrote, "I pour my heart and soul out to you and all you have to say is your favorite TV show and you have to go the gym? Well, I'm looking for a real relationship with a woman who is open and honest and has something meaningful to say, like her feelings. Good luck meeting someone."

Before you take it personally or take your ad down, realize that most men are used to chatting up a storm online with non-*Rules* girls who tell men virtually everything but their bra size by the second e-mail, so of course he is going to think you are a snob. Do not argue or get into a whole big discussion. Just say, "Sorry, but I am new to this," even if you have been cyberdating for five years.

But also realize this is probably not going to go anywhere and you may not want to e-mail him again. Any man
who shows this much anger in a second e-mail to a stranger
is scary and will probably be just as angry in real life. Some
women, not knowing about "buyer beware" and *The Rules,*
will answer back with apologies or explanations, thus pro-
longing a bad e-mail relationship.

Other women who are angry themselves may write a
nasty e-mail back, such as, "I wouldn't be open and honest
with a nut like you for all the tea in China. Seek help!"

Both responses are wrong. *Rules* girls are neither door-
mats nor bad-tempered. They take out their frustrations in
therapy or at the gym, not online. They say nothing if they
have nothing nice to say. So delete is best in this case; there's
no point e-mailing back because you are not dealing with a
full playing deck here.

An emotionally sound man would make plans to have
drinks on date zero and chat with you then, knowing that it
could potentially lead to dinner on a second date, where of
course he would find out more about you. When a man has
this many issues in his first or second e-mail, you know he
may not be reasonable.

An angry man will find fault with whatever you write.
One woman wrote, "I like your profile" in her first e-mail,
but then waited 24 hours to send him another e-mail
because she was trying to do *The Rules.* She got this e-mail
back: "I waited a long time to hear from you. Are you interested in a relationship or not? P.S. I am not a profile. I am a
man with flesh and blood, hopes and dreams . . . If you are
into playing games, I am not interested. Do me a favor, stay
home, and take yourself out of the gene pool."

Another man wrote, "I am offended that you don't want to meet for dinner. In other words, you want me to drive forty-five minutes each way to watch you sip a soda? Are you anorexic or antisocial or what? I like to meet a woman over a nice long dinner. Think about it."

These get an automatic delete, too, or a "Maybe this isn't going to work . . . good luck" response. But do not argue with these men. A normal man would be trying to make a good impression in his first few e-mails and would never complain about the drive nor be cruel or accusatory in his response to you, someone he has never met! Some women, not knowing *The Rules,* would think they had to respond to this with long, placating e-mails in hopes this will dissipate his anger. Some women may even change their plans and agree to dinner for a first date or even meet him halfway. *Rules* girls do not waste time arguing or agreeing to meet with angry men. Delete/next!

7. Delete e-mails that are sexual. Any man who talks about sex (favorite positions), asks if you are kinky, or uses words like *breasts* and other body parts in his e-mails is just looking for sex. Enough said. Delete/next!

8. Don't get hung up on the one-time caller. If a man answers your ad or Instant Messages you first in a chat room, gets your number, and only calls you once, don't call him back or spend time figuring out why he didn't call again. We find that when an online guy calls once and doesn't call back or doesn't even follow-up with an e-mail such as, "Hi, tried calling you but you weren't home . . . hope we can chat soon," then he wasn't that interested to begin with.

Remember, you are meeting men online where part of the fun for some of them is looking at pictures and responding to lots of different women so that their e-mail box is full every day, without wanting, necessarily, to bond with one special woman. Answering ads and Instant Messaging you does not require as much effort as walking over to you in a club, buying you a drink, or asking you to dance, and getting your phone number, so the fallout is bigger online and men poof! easier. The return on investment here is smaller, but don't let that stop you from being online. Have a thick skin, don't take it personally.

9. Ignore men who won't take no for an answer. If you ignored or said "not interested/no thanks" to a man who responded to your ad and yet he keeps e-mailing you or Instant Messaging you to reconsider and e-mail him back, don't. Just keep ignoring him until he goes away. Some men are relentless or pathological and think that if they keep hounding you—for example, "Did you get my last e-mail?" or "What's the matter? Not good-looking enough for you?" or "Are you ever going to e-mail me back?" or "I'm still waiting"—you will eventually cave in.

Do not think you are being rude to keep ignoring them. Do not even *worry* what they think. Do not be flattered either; they are probably harassing six other women on the same service. Many online dating services provide a "decline contact" feature, but if he already has your e-mail address, it will be harder to cut communication. They are men who simply cannot take no for an answer and no one you want to chat with or meet. They will eventually tire of contacting you and answer other ads.

10. Most important, use delete/next! if you are unsure about him for any reason, or your gut says no. It used to be (10 years ago) that everyone in cyberspace was considered a potential molester or murderer. Today we know that is far from the truth. Very normal professional men and women are meeting and mating online all the time. However, if you have any doubts about the credibility of the guy you are e-mailing, if he refuses to give you his work and home numbers (which you should call when he is not there to make sure he is real), if he doesn't say what he does for a living, or is evasive, or insists on knowing where you live or work (do not give this out), trust your inner voice and don't meet him.

Rule 13

Don't Waste Time on Time-Wasters

As a *Rules* girl, you do things differently than other women online. As we've said earlier, your ad and your answers to the questionnaire are going to be shorter than the average woman's online, but you know it doesn't matter.

So if a man writes you, "I read your ad, it seems we have a lot in common, you seem interesting, but I still would like to know more about you," you file it in the back of your head that he may be a "time-waster." A time-waster is a man who asks too many questions but never asks you out. For example, he might e-mail you and ask, "If you were a color, what would it be? If you could meet anyone, dead or alive, who would it be and why?" This man is probably looking for a friend he can philosophize with, not a woman to take out on a date.

This is a new kind of junkie—*the man who needs to know more online.* With the advent of the Internet, he can be online all day and night. He is able to learn more about the world, politics, economics, coin collecting, rare artifacts, and tons of other topics, in addition to meeting women. So the Internet is a wonderful and exciting place for the time-waster. He can meet all kinds of people and talk about all kinds of things that never existed for him before. Online dating services and chat rooms have opened up a whole new impersonal world for him where he can be with people 24 hours a day—but never with anyone in particular—and that's exactly how he likes it!

You can pick this guy out. He will just want to e-mail back and forth or Instant Message you, he may want more than one photo, he may want to see a body shot in addition to your head shot, and then maybe one of you and your dog. As a *Rules* girl and a CUAO, you don't have time for all this. Besides, you know that all a man really needs to know to ask you on a date are a few e-mail exchanges, one photo, and your approximate age—the same facts he would have if he met you in a bar, walked over to you, and said, "Hey, how are you tonight? My friends are leaving but I think you're attractive. I was wondering if I could get your number and meet you for a drink sometime."

The man who has to know why your last relationship/ marriage ended and what you are looking for in future relationships, and your goals before he can ask you out is just a time-waster. He's a man who likes to chat online, period.

He is not necessarily a bad guy, although you may find out later on if you continue to chat with him that he is dealing with psychological problems, or is a loner/genius type and that is why he is content to get to know you online but nowhere else. But he looks good on the outside, so many women are initially deceived by his packaging.

In fact, he may be very cute and have a great job, invariably one that requires him to travel so he has a great reason why he can't ask you out. He may have relatives who visit him or whom he visits on weekends or sick parents he has to take care of, or some other unusual situation in his life, thus making it impossible for him to see you on Saturday nights or to meet you at all. This is how he devises it because online contact is fulfilling enough for him, that's all he really wants. This type is not really looking for a relationship although he may say he is and may even think he is. He may not be married or even have a girlfriend, so you may think, "Hey, I have a live one here," but he exists only online and nowhere else as far as women are concerned.

At first, you might think that such a man is a potential best friend. After all, he seems interested in who you are, your innermost thoughts and feelings, and why your last few relationships didn't work out. You've never met him and yet he asks you about your day more than your own mother does. This kind of guy doesn't like brief ads; why should he? There's no fodder for his addiction. He doesn't really plan on having a relationship with you and may not even plan on meeting you—you are merely interesting to him, like a case study of women or a form of entertainment.

As a *Rules* girl who doesn't have long ads and doesn't answer a lot of questions, you may think you are a challenge to him and you may be thrilled when he writes, "Your ad was nice but too short, I'd like to know more about you." Buyer beware! Don't fall for his lines! His e-mails are not a means to an end (dates) but an end in themselves. His appetite for information is insatiable. No matter how much you tell him, he always has one more question, and then one more. So don't change your ad or bare your soul in subsequent e-mails by telling him what you are looking for in a man or any of the other 20 deep questions he may ask.

After reading this chapter you will hopefully be able to pick out the time-waster in a second. When you write back to him saying, "There's really not much more to tell"—a way to indicate that you're only interested in dating—he either doesn't respond or he puts you down with angry and insincere e-mails like, "Are you really that quiet? How do you expect me to learn about you if you have nothing to say?" You want to say, "Hey, you can ask me out," but it won't work with this type, because this man is happily in a solo relationship with himself.

You just have to move on. It may be hard to forget him if he is very cute, a good writer, or interesting. You may check your e-mail every day hoping that he wrote you again and asked you out. This will probably be a waste of your time. Remember, his need to know about you is like that of a scientist doing research in a laboratory, not that of a man becoming enamored of *you*, not a man falling in love with *you*.

Rule 14

Don't Force the Relationship from E-mail to Phone

Online dating is like a chess game. The man makes the first move and you follow in kind. But do not try to dictate how *he* plays the game.

Like it or not, these days more men are using e-mail than phone to communicate with women and even ask them out. Frankly, this is driving some women crazy. If you are dating someone who e-mails you several times a week and only calls once or twice a week, you may be one of these women. It doesn't help, of course, that your mother and friends tell you that it's not a real relationship unless he calls more often. Even though you know you are a couple, have weekly Saturday night dates, and everything is fine, part of you thinks they may have a point. And when your manicurist suggested recently that he's just a sex buddy if he doesn't call every day, you couldn't help but wonder if she was right.

Like most women, you may want us to tell you how to

"move the relationship to more phone" without actually coming out and saying "call me." You may want us to tell you if it is OK to accept a date by e-mail. These seem to be the burning questions in just about every online consultation we do.

We understand how you feel. As women, we understand the preference for the phone, we understand that calls are more personal, and that e-mail can be businesslike, even cold. It's fun when dating to check Caller ID and see your boyfriend's number on it. However, we are here to tell you this: Times have changed. Cyberspace has taken over. *It is not any less of a relationship if a man prefers to e-mail you;* it's just a technological preference.

The fact is, some men like the computer and some men like the phone. For some men, e-mailing is just easier and more efficient than the phone. As a man would say, e-mail "gets the job done!" Remember, the average guy has clients he must call, his stockbroker, lawyer, accountant, car dealer, plumber, realtor, mortgage broker, perhaps an ex-wife or children, and who knows who else, so if he can e-mail you instead of calling sometimes, that makes his life easier. There may be other reasons he prefers e-mail: He doesn't have to worry about catching you at a bad time, such as when you are at work or busy at home. And he doesn't have to worry about making conversation, like what to say after "How about a comedy club this Saturday night?"

As far as *The Rules* is concerned, this e-mail-versus-calling thing is much ado about nothing. They're both a means to an end—to set up Saturday night dates—not an end in themselves. E-mail is no less than a phone call *as long as he is asking you out on dates every week in advance of Wednesday.* The fact is, e-mails *are* phone calls.

So to answer your question: If he e-mails you by Wednesday for a Saturday night date, you can e-mail him back "yes." The guy who is e-mailing you in advance for the weekend is not the one to worry about; it's the guy who calls you on Friday afternoon for Saturday night! Do not get hung up on the seeming superiority of calling versus e-mailing. Stop talking to your judgmental friends about your relationship. It could be that your friends who dated before the Internet don't have a clue about e-mail and thus think it is an inferior form of communication. Or maybe they're just phone snobs. Whatever. Hopefully you will do *The Rules* on this guy who likes to e-mail you and he will propose and then you can invite all these skeptics to your wedding and that will be the end of that!

As a *Rules* girl, you go with the flow, you let a man take the lead. You don't try to force e-mails into phone calls. That is telling a man what to do and trying to make something happen, which *never* works.

Women who are intent on "moving the relationship to the phone" can get obsessed and ruin otherwise good relationships. Here are some typical e-mail hints women have sent men to get them to call more.

"I'm not a good speller . . . why don't you call me?"

"I'm getting tired of typing . . . why don't you call me?"

"Did I give you my cell number? Here it is again . . ."

"My nails break when I type."

"My computer is acting up . . . oops, they are booting me off again."

"I miss your voice."

"I forgot what you sound like . . ."

"Is your phone broken?"

"Do you own a phone?"

"Wanna have phone sex?"

Avoid dropping hints like these—especially the last one!

Emily, 33, is one of these types who became obsessed with being called. She met Mike, 37, at a singles weekend. He asked her to dance and they spent some of the weekend together. When it was time to go home, Mike, a stockbroker, asked Emily, a human resources manager, for her e-mail address. She gave him her e-mail address as well as her phone number scribbled on the back of her business card. He e-mailed her a few days later saying, "Hi, had a great time. Maybe we can get together again soon, maybe this weekend?" She e-mailed him back the next morning, "Would love to! I'm home tonight after 7 P.M. Why don't you call me so I can give you directions?" He called and they made a dinner date.

After their first date, Mike started asking Emily out at the end of their dates. He also followed up with weekly phone calls and e-mails every few days such as "Can't wait to see you Saturday night. Any ideas for what to do?" or "How's your day going?" Occasionally, he would e-mail her a joke.

Emily was happy. Mike was good-looking and charming. He picked her up every Saturday night and took her to nice restaurants. He bought her flowers twice and a bracelet for her birthday. He made her laugh on dates, and was a good conversationalist as well as attentive and reliable.

But there was one thing that bothered Emily no end— Mike didn't call . . . enough! She complained to her friends that he called "only once a week" and that it was a sign of his lack of commitment on some level. Emily loved to talk on the phone and she had never had a boyfriend who didn't call several times a week, sometimes every night. She missed the phone part of the relationship. She was also embarrassed to say no when her friends asked "So did he call last night?" So she was determined to get Mike to call and started dropping hints in her e-mails.

> *"There's a new Middle Eastern restaurant that just opened up in my neighborhood that has belly dancing. It's hard to describe in writing. Can you call me around 9 tonight so I can tell you about it?"*
>
> *"I wrote three proposals this week. I'm tired of typing . . . "*
>
> *"My computer is acting up. Do you think you can call me to walk me through it so I don't lose all my files?"*
>
> *"I have appointments out of the office all week. It's best to reach me on my cell . . . "*
>
> *"I'd like you to be the last person I talk to at the end of the day . . . "*
>
> *"My ex and I used to say good night over the phone every night. It was very romantic . . . "*
>
> *"You don't call enough."*
>
> *"You never call."*
>
> *"Do you hate the phone?"*
>
> *"How often did you call your last girlfriend?"*

She began to complain on dates about the fact that he didn't call more often. He didn't get what the big deal was, but, trying to please her, he called more often one week and then slipped back into e-mails the following week. The fact was, he was busy trying to build up a client base and found it easier to e-mail her than call. She insisted that there was more to it, a sign of commitment-phobia. They argued on dates about it and sometimes didn't even kiss good night.

Like most men, Mike just preferred e-mail because it was efficient. He liked Emily and enjoyed their weekly dates and e-mail exchanges, but he was not a big caller. But the hints never ended. Suddenly dating Emily had become work. What he really wanted to do after a long day of trading and listening to screaming clients was play basketball or zone out in front of the TV. Mike repeatedly told her that he really didn't have anything to say that warranted more phone calls and that they could talk on dates. But that didn't satisfy her. Emily was relentless.

The straw that broke the camel's back came on an all-day bicycle trip. Mike had planned the trip for weeks and even drove 45 minutes to borrow his sister's helmet for Emily. Rather than appreciate his effort, Emily went on a tirade during their bike ride about his lack of phone calls. She still felt something was seriously wrong and told him so. "I just don't feel cared for when you don't call me every day," she yelled from five feet away as she was trying to catch up with him. Mike didn't say a word. When the day ended, he simply helped Emily off with her helmet, dropped her off at her apartment, and rode away. He never called or e-mailed her again. That was the end of the relationship.

Emily was devastated and called and e-mailed Mike for weeks afterward but to no avail. He was done with the relationship.

We are telling you this to show you what happens when you push a man to do something he doesn't want to do. He rebels. You can't tell a man what to do. You can't demand that a man call instead of e-mail, or tell him how to ask you out or how to love you. You can try, of course, but it won't work. Fighting with a man about it will only make him call and e-mail less. You just have to say, "If everything else is good, who cares if he e-mails or calls?"

Men are not stupid. They know most women would rather

get a phone call. So if you drop enough hints, they may call you once or twice extra to make you happy. But this is like telling a man you want jewelry for your birthday. You may very well get it, but it won't be from his heart, he will just be complying with your wishes and maybe trying to avoid a fight. Better to get what you get than tell a man what to do. In the long run, you won't be happy if it wasn't his idea to call.

We know what you are thinking. How are you going to get to know a man if you don't talk on the phone? After all, e-mails back and forth are not exactly like a spontaneous, live phone conversation. Our answer is you can talk to him on dates and weekends. What a concept! But think about it, before cell phones, beepers, pagers, and computers took over communication as we know it, that's how men and women got to know each other. True, couples spoke on the phone, but we doubt they spoke 12 times a day or for two hours. Phone calls, like e-mails, are just a means to an end, the end being spending time together. Do not think of the phone as the be-all and end-all of a relationship.

Besides, there are many benefits to a man e-mailing instead of calling you. It is actually easier to do *The Rules* with e-mail than with the phone. You don't have to worry about returning his calls and catching him at a bad time, you don't have to worry about staying on the phone too long (*Rules* girls get off the phone in 10 minutes) or talking too much or filling in those awkward silences. You can think about what you want to say in response to his e-mail and take a day to say it, thus avoiding saying something silly or needy. Even better, you can read his e-mails over and over again, as many times a day as you want!

Diane was the exact opposite of Emily. A *Rules* girl, she was so busy she hardly noticed whether guys were calling or e-mailing her. She just knew she was booked on Saturday night dates all summer and that was good enough for her.

Diane, 29, met Jeffrey, 35, in the fall at the opening of an art gallery where she was the manager. Jeffrey was in the market for art work. He asked Diane about a particular artist and then asked if they could continue their conversation over dinner that evening. She politely turned him down for dinner, saying she had plans. *(Rules* girls don't accept on-the-spot dates.) He had her business card and e-mailed her the next day, "Had fun talking to you last night, are you free this Saturday night for dinner? "

Diane waited 24 hours and then e-mailed him back, "Hi. Dinner Saturday night sounds great."

Jeffrey asked Diane out every week by e-mail. He explained that he had just bought a laptop computer and was addicted. Sometimes he asked her out at the end of a date and would call to confirm the date or occasionally chat, but he definitely e-mailed more than called. Truth be told, sometimes she deliberately did not respond to an e-mail so that he would be forced to call her.

But in her heart, she knew it didn't matter whether a man asked her by phone, e-mail, skywriting, or Federal Express. She knew that as long as she did *The Rules,* the technology didn't matter. She knew he wasn't going to profess his love or propose by e-mail, so what difference did it make if he said, "How about a movie and dinner?" by phone or over the Internet? *Rules* girls don't even notice how men contact them. They are easy to be with, not controlling or self-centered.

Jeffrey eventually did propose (in person) and his phone calls became more frequent as they had lots to talk about planning the wedding!

Rule 15

Put Safety First

Safety precautions can never be emphasized enough. To illustrate this point, a couple of years ago we were speaking at a seminar in Toronto when a woman in the audience told us how excited she was about meeting this great guy she had been corresponding with on the Internet. She said he was going to pick her up at her apartment and then they were going to drive together to a nearby museum.

We gasped! We immediately stopped the seminar and focused on her for the next 15 minutes. "This man shouldn't know where you live and you shouldn't be getting into a car with him. You don't know him from a hole in the wall. Call him immediately and tell him you have to change plans. Take your own car, meet him at the museum, and do not get in his car for any reason," we told her. She argued with us and said that, after all, she knew where he worked. We asked if she had ever called him at work (we advise women to call a man at the number he gives them when they think he's not there just to see if he is real) or knew anyone who knew him. She said no. We said, if you get in his car you are taking your life into your own hands. She agreed to follow our advice and changed her plans.

The most important safety rule: *Always meet in a public place no matter how well or how long you have been e-mailing each other.* Do not go to his place and do not let him come to yours. He should not even know where you live!

Here are 10 other safety tips:

1. Make sure you have an unlisted number. Otherwise, someone can find out your home address on the Internet. This is known as reverse lookup: He enters your phone number and it returns your full name and address, as well as a map to your place. Also do a quick check that your address isn't on the Internet already. You can go to the following sites and look yourself up:

http://people.yahoo.com/
http://anywho.com/

2. Get Caller ID. This is just a smart idea for any single woman. If you get a pest continually calling you, you know not to pick up the phone. Also, it reveals a lot of information about the guys that do call. For example, if they always call from work, a cell phone, or a pay phone, they may be married or involved with someone.

3. Do not give men your home or work numbers. Just give them your cell phone number or a voice-mail number at first.

4. Block yourself by hitting *67 when you call men from home, otherwise they can hit *69 and get your number or see your full name as well as the number if they have Caller ID.

5. Never use your real name as your screen name. Do not tell men your last name, what car you drive, or where you work. For example, do not say "I work for Citibank on Main Street." Just say "I work at a bank."

6. For the date, suggest a place that is in an area that you know very well and that is near your home but not around the corner so he can't follow you there afterward. Try to pick a place that is always crowded and where parking is well lit—not some bistro in a dark alley. If there is valet parking, use it. Do not meet for dinner as that could take hours, but for a quick drink, coffee, or ice cream. Date zero should not be more than two hours. And no matter how great it is going, do not agree to leave your safe meeting place to do something afterward, such as a cappuccino, a movie, or a walk in the park, as he could lead you into his car. Once you are in his car, he can lock the doors and take you anywhere he wants. It would be insane to get into his car. If he wants to spend more time with you, he has to ask you out on another date.

7. Tell your friends or the most paranoid members of your family that you are meeting a man that you know from the Internet and give them the date, time, and place of the date and any information about him, such as his name, home, work, and cell numbers as well as his e-mail address

and photo if possible. Tell them the date will be about an hour or two and that you will call them when you get home. Tell them to call your cell phone if they have not heard from you by a certain time. Don't forget to bring your cell phone with you on the date just in case.

8. If you feel uncomfortable or are getting bad vibes at any point during the date, say you have to go—and leave! Do not worry about being rude.

9. Do not let him walk you to your car. Do not let him see where you are going. Try to leave separately. If you do walk out together, drive in the opposite direction until you have lost him and then go home. Then immediately call your family or friends.

10. Hopefully this tip is not necessary, but never leave your drink unattended. You never know what your date can drop into your drink that may make you prey to his wishes. And, of course, don't have more than one drink because it's harder to do *The Rules* and make safe choices if you do.

Remember, safety comes first!

Rule 16

Don't Ad-Interrogate on Dates

Remember in our first book how we told you not to open up too fast on dates, to talk about light things like the restaurant, work, and movies because, after all, dating isn't therapy? Well, the same applies to dates with men you meet online, only there's a new twist here and a bigger temptation to delve into relationship talk. Women now have men's ads at their disposal and are talking about them and even interrogating men about them on dates, which is the latest form of *Rule*-breaking behavior. Here's one example of how a promising beginning (he answered her ad) turned into a nightmare via ad-interrogation.

Rachel, 34, an art director at an ad agency, had just ended a two-year relationship, put up an ad, and was thrilled to get more than 75 responses. After screening heavily, one in particular caught her attention. It was from Gary, a business journalist. Gary's e-mail to her was just so clever and when she looked up his profile and saw his photo, she thought, "Wow!"

She forwarded it to her three best friends and wrote, "This is my kind of guy!" After a few e-mails back and forth, they made a date.

A week later, they met for dinner. As they sat down, Gary smiled because Rachel was even prettier than her picture and he was relieved because his last few online dates were disappointing to say the least. He'd had a long day at work and thought as he ordered a drink, "This should be fun!" He looked at the menu but did not say anything. Rachel barely looked at the menu—food was the last thing on her mind! She was more interested in figuring out what to say to this almost perfect stranger. So as Gary was being served his drink, she decided the best way to get the conversation going and also show him how interested she was, was to bring up facts from his ad.

"So, let me see . . . you said you live in Connecticut, that you have two children and are divorced two years. Your favorite color is blue, your favorite sport is skiing, and you have a dog, am I right?" she asked, smiling.

Gary was relaxing and deciding whether he was going to get the chicken special or shrimp over rice with sautéed vegetables. His doctor had just told him his cholesterol was high and to stay away from too much fat. Should he get the shrimp steamed or would that be too plain? That's what he was thinking.

"Yes, everything you said is correct. You have a good memory," he answered. Rachel continued to chatter away about his ad and then decided it was time to get beneath the surface, to really know this guy, to see what makes him tick. So she decided to ask him questions about the essay part of the questionnaire.

"So I remember your saying in your essay that communication is the most important thing in a relationship. I know self-help books say that men don't like to talk that much and my ex never wanted to talk, that's the main reason we broke up . . . so did you really mean that?"

Gary looked up from his drink and said, "Did I say that? I don't remember." Then he decided that he better say he meant it just to keep things pleasant. "Yes, I feel communication is very important."

Rachel continued to ask more questions about his ad as their main course was being served and that's when Gary lost both his appetite for dinner and his interest in Rachel. He excused himself to go to the bathroom. Rachel thought he was taking a long time. When he came back to the table, his beeper went off almost immediately and he made a quick cell phone call and told her that something came up and that he was very sorry but he really had to get going. He got the check, thanked her for a lovely evening, and left.

Rachel e-mailed him the next morning, "Thanks for dinner, hope everything is OK," and signed it with a smiley face. When she never heard back from him, she e-mailed us to find out what went wrong.

Believe it or not, Rachel is *not* the first woman we have heard of who memorized a man's profile and then went over his answers point-by-point over drinks or dinner, as if she were hiring a nanny or an executive assistant!

We are not being naive. We know that you, like every other woman on earth, read his ad, and you know you read his ad, and men probably figure you read their ads. But the whole point is to pretend on dates that you *didn't* read their ads, that at most you scanned them. Quoting a man's comments shows too much interest and intensity. It will scare any man away. Remembering everything about his career, his income, the ages of his two kids, and the fact that he likes to ski in Aspen once a year sounds like you are planning the wedding.

Pretend you have amnesia. Pretend you had five dates that week and can barely remember anyone's name, much less their hobbies. Try to forget you even met him online and that there was even an ad. It's all a blur. You could have met him at a bar or an office party. You'd have to think about it. You are *so* busy!

If you go on dates like a reporter grilling a politician or a celebrity, trust us, what happened to Rachel will happen to you. We told Rachel that her interrogating him about his ad was just too much and such a turn-off that he probably beeped himself!

Men and women are as different in the online world as they are in real life. As far as questionnaires go, men very often write what they think women want to hear, sprinkling in words like "communication" and "soul mate" and "connection" even though they may have had a one-night stand the night before!

Of course, there are some men who fill out these forms carefully and write down their relationship thoughts in earnest, but even they would never expect anyone to remember the ad and grill them over it, especially not on the first few dates.

Another woman, Mindy, who also e-mailed us for advice, went right for the jugular on her first date with Dave: "I noticed you said in your ad that what you learned from past relationships is to never try to change another person. Was this an issue in your marriage or a past relationship?" Like most women, Mindy loved to ask about past relationships because she thought that if she knew what went wrong with an ex, she had a window into the soul of her new prey.

Dave, who was sipping a glass of wine, gulped. He could barely remember writing that, but since it sounded good, he agreed that he wrote it and said he meant it and that it kind of applied to every woman he'd ever been with, so as to avoid talking about his ex-wife. "I believe in accepting people 'just the way they are,' like the Billy Joel song says. Yes, I think that's very important," he said.

When Mindy ran out of material from his ad, she added insult to injury by quoting from her own ad. "I don't know if you remember my ad, but I said that I was looking for someone I have a lot in common with. . . . My last boyfriend loved sports and was glued to the TV. I hate sports and hardly watch TV. I love to dance, he didn't. We had little in common. . . . So I don't want to make that mistake again. What do you think?" All this after knowing him for only 30 minutes!

She went on and on about the importance of spending time together and shared interests. Dave, like most men, had been thinking visually. He wasn't thinking about their ads at all. He had been thinking what it would be like to kiss her and caress her long hair. He was thinking about how her hair bounced as she walked into the restaurant with her long sexy legs.

If it were up to Mindy, she would have printed out both ads, put them next to each other, side by side, and checked off what they had in common. Unbeknownst to Mindy, Dave thought the whole essay thing was ridiculous. Like many men, he read online ads like Victoria's Secret catalogues. Having just put in a 12-hour day as a stockbroker, he just wanted to meet a nice girl who had relationship potential for a couple of drinks and dinner and have some fun for two or three hours. He didn't think he was going on a job interview. Now all he wanted to do was go home! He got the check and got away from Mindy as fast as he could.

We know that you don't want to waste time, and we know that you have your issues and feel entitled to know more about this guy because you have access to written information about him. But interrogating him is not the way to do it! Be smart. The best way to learn about a man is to let him steer the conversation, to see what he likes to talk about, to observe how he treats you (opens the door, offers to pick up the check, and so on) and how he treats the waitress (if the food comes and it is not exactly the way he wanted it, will he either let it go or be nice about returning it?). What should be quietly going on in your head is: Does he seem interested in you? Do you like him? Are you getting good feelings? Does he want to extend the date? Do you feel he is going to ask you out again?

Remember, love is a spark and cannot be figured out by a list! Some of the best romantic relationships would never have happened if the couples had to check off a list of questions on mutual hobbies, political orientations, and philosophies. Trying to find out who he is with deep questions is useless anyway because anybody can say anything about anything just as anybody can write anything in questionnaires. We believe you should just show up, put on your best smile, listen—listen a lot—and be patient. Patience is a virtue, and sooner or later all your questions will be answered.

Rule 17

Don't Have Sex on Dates One, Two, or Three

E-mail intimacy is never the same as actually dating a man. Only on dates can you see how he behaves, what his moods are, what his character is like, and what his feelings for you seem to be. A man's e-mails may be nice, but he may not be! So to think you can sleep with an online guy the first time you meet him just because you have been e-mailing each other for two months is insane and rushing things, to say the least.

First of all, we do not suggest you get into an ongoing e-mail "relationship" before you actually meet a man face-to-face. E-mail is only words on a screen. You don't really know him; he may be lying about things; he could be involved with someone or just a player. Many romances have blossomed on the Internet and then poofed! in person because the man lied or there was no chemistry. You cannot tell if you have real chemistry with a man on the computer. As we stated in *Rule*

11, if a man does not suggest meeting after four e-mails (within two weeks to a month at the latest), it's delete/next! If it's a long-distance relationship, it might take a little bit longer for him to visit you, but not more than three months.

We believe you should then date a man for several months before sleeping with him, even if he writes like Hemingway and you think you are falling in love. Why? Because you don't want to sleep with a man until you are pretty sure it is meaningful. Physical intimacy should happen slowly over a period of six to eight dates, not impulsively on the first or second date, no matter how you feel or how long you've been reading his e-mails and think you "know" him.

No one knows this better than Jill, 38, a makeup artist from Michigan. Andy, 44, an insurance agent from Florida, answered her ad and thus began a fast and furious e-mail and Instant Message courtship that went on for two months before they met. He Instant Messaged her one night and the conversation went like this:

InsuranceGuy44: *Hey beautiful . . . you have a great smile.*
PrettyGal38: *Thanks. What's your name?*
InsuranceGuy44: *Andy, what's yours?*
PrettyGal38: *Jill. My brother's name is Andy.*
InsuranceGuy44: *So how's the dating going? Meet anyone good?*
PrettyGal38: *Not yet, just put my ad up.*
InsuranceGuy44: *How many responses did you get, 5,000?*
PrettyGal38: *Thanks, I wish. About 100.*
InsuranceGuy44: *I'm sure a good-looking girl like you doesn't have to worry about meeting a guy. What happened with your husband?*

PrettyGal38: *He's an alcoholic and a womanizer. What about your wife?*

InsuranceGuy44: *Just grew apart.*

Jill and Andy spoke every day like this and told each other everything about their exes, their kids, their past relationships, career stuff, hopes, dreams, and hobbies. In a matter of weeks, Jill already knew his favorite cologne, favorite baseball team, favorite book, and his dream car, a two-seater Lexus, which he planned to buy after the lease on his Jeep was up.

After dozens of Instant Messages and e-mails back and forth, Andy finally suggested they meet:

InsuranceGuy44: *The weather is fantastic in Florida right now. It must be freezing in Michigan. Why don't you come down here and visit me? I love chatting with you, I can't wait to meet you.*

Jill would have preferred that Andy visit her or that he at least offer to pay for her plane ticket. But she figured that there was a holiday weekend coming up and she had frequent flier mileage and a cousin in Florida she could also visit, so why not?

PrettyGal38: *That sounds great.*

InsuranceGuy44: *Can't wait, pretty gal!*

Andy was supposed to pick up Jill at the airport that Friday afternoon, but a last-minute business meeting held him up, so he called Jill on her cell phone and told her to take a cab to his office and that he would pay for it. She waited in the lobby of his company for 45 minutes, holding a small bottle of his favorite cologne, as a little getting-to-know-you gift, hoping he would look like his hunky photo.

Unfortunately, Andy was not as good-looking as his photo, which must have been 10 years old. He had a pot belly and looked much older, but she loved his e-mail personality and decided to overlook his appearance and the fact that he forgot to pay her back for the cab.

Andy picked a romantic restaurant for dinner, opened doors, pulled Jill's chair out for her, and then ordered an expensive bottle of wine. Andy's compliments flowed like the wine. "You are much prettier in person," he told her. "I can't believe no one has grabbed you yet." After a few too many drinks, Jill found Andy more and more attractive. He was attentive and a great conversationalist. She thought she could kiss him after all.

After dinner, Andy suggested a nightclub for drinks and dancing and then invited her to his place "to see the view." Jill said OK, thinking she would stay for an hour and then take a cab to her cousin's apartment. But one thing led to another. They started kissing, then making out on his couch, and before she knew it, they were having sex. Andy told Jill he felt that they really connected and that she was "unbelievably sexy." Jill was in heaven.

Jill blew off her cousin, and she and Andy stayed in bed all weekend, having sex, laughing and talking, and ordering bagels for breakfast and Chinese food for dinner. Andy talked about visiting Michigan soon, leaving Jill no doubt in her mind that this was not a one-night stand. But while she was fantasizing about the future of their long-distance relationship, Andy was already thinking about his next conquest: FunGirl41 from San Diego who would be visiting him next week. Andy thought online dating was heaven on earth. All he had to do was send out a few of the same kinds of e-mails to assorted women all over the country, throw compliments their way, and then follow up with some erotic Instant Message sessions, and they were happy to hop on a plane and have sex with him! What an unbelievable deal! Of course, he never e-mailed women in Florida, preferring women out of state who would not be able to check up on him.

Andy went out to get a newspaper, cigarettes, and some groceries. He told Jill to make herself at home and that he would be back in 20 minutes.

Jill walked around his apartment in his bathrobe, feeling very wife-y. When Andy wasn't back in 20 minutes, she decided to log onto his computer and check her mail. She noticed some printouts on his desk of flirtatious Instant Message conversations to "FunGirl41" in California and "Vixen37" in Chicago and decided to check his filing cabinet to see what else there was. She found dozens of e-mails to seven different women all over the country, either asking them to visit him or thanking them for an "unbelievable" weekend! Every e-mail sounded like Andy's e-mails to her, beginning with "Hey beautiful" and "I can't believe someone hasn't grabbed you yet."

Jill felt like a fool. She'd flown to Florida, had sex with him six times in three days, and just realized it was nothing! Andy told her she was special and she believed him, only to find out that he had a girl in every port and that she was just one of many.

When Andy walked in the door, she screamed, "Who's FunGirl41 and why is she coming here next week if you're e-mailing me everyday and sleeping with me? And who's Vixen37? How many women are you sleeping with anyway?"

Andy was furious that she'd gone through his stuff. "What are you, a spy? We're not exactly married . . ."

Then he tried lying, "Those are old e-mails."

When she checked the dates and saw they were recent, he 'fessed up, "Look, I like you a lot, I'm just not really looking to settle down with one person right now. We can still see each other if you want."

Jill was so hurt all she could say was "Not on your life!" She called her cousin, then called a cab, got dressed in a heartbeat, and left his apartment, crying all the way to the airport. What a nightmare! They had been corresponding with each other, every day for two months and knew everything about each other, or so he said. She'd bought him cologne. She'd slept with him. And it was all a big nothing. Jill had believed his adoring e-mails—and long, passionate Instant Message sessions several times a week—and got burnt. She thought that e-mail intimacy equaled true intimacy, that you can "know" a person online, but she found out otherwise. Andy was nothing more than a player who broke her heart and wasted her time.

As Jill and other women we know are finding out, an e-mail relationship can be pure fantasy—it's *nothing*—until you meet and spend time with a man. Any man can write anything in an e-mail. Any man can say he is falling in love with you, any man can say that he is kind and faithful, but only through in-person dating can you see if he is what he says he is.

Only through real-life dating can you see if he looks like his photo.

Only through real-life dating can you see if his behavior measures up to his words. Only on dates can you see if his face lights up or if he seems to feel a spark when he's with you. That look cannot be captured in 20 e-mails. A man can say in an e-mail that he loves your smile and thinks about you when he sleeps at night, but does he feel that way in person? E-mails are terrific for meeting new men and setting up dates, but it's the dates that really count. While e-mails can tell you a lot about a man, dates are the only way to get to know him and to tell if he truly has feelings for you—and you for him. *Real chemistry between a couple only happens in person, not online.*

Meeting him in person, you may find that he's older, heavier, or his hair is thinner than in his photo. Or maybe he's gorgeous and even nicer than his e-mails. *It doesn't matter.* To think you can sleep with a man just because you've created some e-mail intimacy is crazy. You don't really know him yet.

First of all, if you're doing *The Rules,* you won't allow an e-mail relationship to develop before you meet a man. You won't e-mail each other 42 times before you meet—just four times until he asks you out. If he lives out of state, maybe a few more times than that. Whether local or long-distance, your e-mails to him won't be seductive and flirty, but factual, for example "I am 38, an immigration lawyer, newly divorced, with one daughter. I love Chinese food, kick-boxing, and Woody Allen movies." You won't write anything like "I love your sexy eyes" or "Your biceps are a real turn-on." In other words, no e-mail foreplay!

Whether you've met a man online or off, whether you've been communicating by phone, e-mail, or carrier pigeon, you should still date a man at least four times before sleeping with him no matter how you feel! Because until you have spent time with him in person, it could all be fake. Until you know that he is truly interested in you because he is asking you out every week as opposed to his being an excitement junkie or a guy looking for a sexual relationship, it is nothing!

Besides, how do you know that you are not one of many, that he doesn't have several e-mail relationships going on at the same time and that he is not like Andy, having women fly out to meet him and sleeping with each one on the first date? The truth is, you don't know. That is why it is best to wait until he has visited you and made dates with you over a period of a few months to make sure that he is for real and not a fantasy. There is no online shortcut out there: *Real intimacy happens only when you are together!*

Rule 18

"Disappear" in Between Dates

Many of *The Rules* for online dating—such as waiting 24 hours to e-mail a man back, not answering e-mails on weekends, not accepting Instant Messages, and keeping your e-mails short and sweet—discourage excessive contact between you and men. This is a good thing!

We want you to kind of disappear in between dates as much as you can so that the man you are dating almost wonders if he is even dating you. For some strange reason, not knowing exactly where you stand and what you are doing gives men a rush! That is why we believe in playing hard to get and slowly involving a man in your life. It sets the right pace for the relationship, so he isn't overwhelmed.

Slowly involving a man in your life means that you and he are not going out with your parents on the fourth date, or doubling with your friends on a Saturday night on the fifth date. It means you're not e-mailing and Instant Messaging him all day with cute thoughts or forwarding him e-mails from friends and coworkers so as to include him in your life. Under no circumstances are you telling him that you don't see him enough, as if you can't live without a man.

You shouldn't be seeing each other five nights a week after a month, so that after two or three months he has to come up with a reason to get out of this whirlwind courtship. You have to pace the relationship so that it doesn't become too much for him and he ends up wondering how he got himself in so deep so quickly. If he starts to feel overwhelmed, he may panic and run.

Trust us, once a man realizes he is in a relationship with you, he will appreciate less contact because it gives him space to focus on his life and his work, as opposed to being e-mailed by you and e-mailing you back every five minutes. He will enjoy this less-is-more pace of dating, and the reward for both of you is that the relationship will "stick" better, and after a year you'll have built up something real.

Most women (non-*Rules* girls) do not disappear in between dates. On the contrary, they e-mail, call, and Instant Message a man to death to remind him that they exist and that they are in fact in a relationship. These women figure "out of sight, out of mind." They are afraid that if they don't keep constant contact going with him in between dates he will forget them, think about other women in his office, or maybe answer other women's ads online. Actually, the opposite is true. If a man doesn't hear from you constantly in between dates, he will probably think about you more (assuming the relationship started with a *Rules* beginning—he spoke to or e-mailed you first and pursued you). He may even appreciate the lack of constant e-mails.

Men still want what they can't have and that's what makes them different from women. If a man sees you on long, wonderful dates with lots of intimacy and then gets all these warm, loving e-mails, calls, and Instant Messages during the week, what incentive does he have to become committed to and marry you? None! But if you seem to disappear during the week and he doesn't know exactly what you are doing and what you are thinking or feeling about him and the relationship, you will seem mysterious and interesting to him and your dates will be more special.

Now you may be wondering, how will I know how his office renovation is going and how will he know about my new job and so on? Things happen every day in both our lives, why can't we share these things as they occur?

When you are married, you can talk to him every day, but hold back a bit for now. Otherwise, the relationship becomes too casual and familiar and he will get bored. Unfortunately, that's just the way it is!

While we are asking you to hold back on correspondence (including smiley faces, coffee-cup greetings in the morning, and friendship e-mails any time of the day) and calls during the week, don't worry, you will have more than enough time to be yourself on dates. If you are naturally warm and thoughtful, you are warm and thoughtful on dates. He has a dry throat? You ask the waitress to fill up his glass of water and bring him hot tea with lemon. If you are naturally upbeat and complimentary, you tell him a joke or gush about his new tie on the date. But you end the dates first and kind of disappear in between until he asks to see you again.

For most women, this is not easy to do. After a wonderful Saturday night filled with warmth and all the right feelings and ingredients for a relationship, most women naturally want to keep these feelings going. Women feel it goes against nature to wait for the next date to make contact. Men are different. They will spend a weekend playing golf with a friend and then not talk to him again until the next golf game two months later, even if the market dropped and the friend is getting a divorce.

So when we told women in our first book not to call men in between dates, they felt as if we were asking them to stop breathing, but then they had to admit that they loved the results. Men, who are results-oriented, understand this more than women do. How often have you heard a man say "Let's just get the job done?" So if you want results, you can't just do whatever you feel like, but what works long-term. And we can tell you for sure that what works long-term is limiting your contact with a man in between dates.

Without *The Rules*, even the smartest women tend to behave in a way that sabotages the most promising relationships. They don't mean to do that, but that's what happens.

Case in point:

Jane, 51, a therapist, is the kind of person who calls her friends when they are sick, always returns phone calls and never forgets anyone's birthday. Phil, 55, a chiropractor (CuteDoc55), answered her ad (SmartLady51), and they started seeing each other every week. On average, he e-mailed her twice a week and called about once a week to confirm plans. Jane e-mailed him back every time and she also sent him e-mails thanking him for dates, e-mails asking him about his day, and e-mails asking how his son did on his SATs. And when he had a cold, she sent him a feel-good e-mail card. She also cut and pasted together every e-mail they sent to each other for a collage that she gave him for their two-month anniversary! For Phil, it started to become overwhelming.

About six weeks after this, she noticed that his e-mails were less frequent and shorter and when she Instant Messaged him once, he got off first.

"Work is crazy," he said and logged off before she could blink. When she e-mailed him the next day to invite him to her office Christmas party, he e-mailed back, "I'm off the screen for this holiday. . . ."

Jane got hysterical and called a good friend, who told her about *The Rules*. Her friend told her to disappear in between dates, rarely return his e-mails, and to stop being so chatty and concerned. "Don't be *his* therapist!" she advised Jane, the therapist.

Asking Jane to be detached and busy was so against her nature and her profession, but her fear of losing CuteDoc55 with her sweetness and intensity was incentive enough. So she started not responding to his e-mails unless they were about their dates. Sure enough, he e-mailed her that he "Had a great time the other night," which he had never done before. When she didn't respond, she got an "I'm thinking about you" the next morning. The following day, he Instant Messaged her "Where have you been?" She did not Instant Message him back, but e-mailed him 24 hours later, "Hi, sorry, just some computer glitches with our new system. . . . Oops, there it goes again!" and logged off. (Later, her friend told her to block herself so she could not accept Instant Messages and she did that.)

Jane had to admit both strategies worked. That evening, Phil called and asked to see her twice that week, Saturday night for dinner and dancing, and Sunday to go to a basketball game with his son, whom she had never met. Now Jane is sold on *The Rules for Online Dating!*

Pulling back a little like Jane did when Phil became complacent (for example, skipping the holidays) usually works like a charm. But what do you do when a man is behaving really badly, if, for example, he begins skipping Saturday nights, saying he's not sure how he feels or that he needs space, or he hasn't proposed after one-and-a-half to two years of dating? Seeming to disappear in between dates and limiting contact is standard operating procedure for when things are going well between you, but when things are going badly, a more extreme solution is necessary.

We call this the "No Contact" plan. We believe the only way to wake up a wayward guy is to not contact him at all! You must stop seeing him and ignore all calls and e-mails and just let him keep trying to get in touch with you until he changes his tune—stops being complacent, commits, and proposes. When you start getting e-mail flowers or real flowers at your door with a meaningful note about the relationship, then you can pick up the phone or e-mail him back. Until then, nothing!

Here is a perfect example of how No Contact works: Lynn met Matthew, both 35, when he answered her ad online. He thought she was very cute and had no problem asking for her telephone number in his third e-mail. He called her the next day and suggested drinks that Friday night. There was instant attraction on both sides and one date led to another and another. Lynn was totally smitten with Matthew and felt he was "the one." She was also at a place in her life where she wanted to get married sooner rather than later: she felt she had done the dating "scene" enough to last a lifetime. Some of her friends from college were already on their third child.

Having broken *The Rules* in previous relationships, Lynn was one of those "I'll never break *The Rules* again" types. She was so strict, in fact, that their two-year relationship could be described as almost idyllic. From day one, there were weekly dates and follow-up calls and e-mails, romantic presents, and holidays spent together. Lynn did not sleep with Matthew until their ninth date, was easy to be with, and busy with her own life in between dates. She agreed that "disappearing" a bit in between dates only made Matthew more interested and gave her more time for her friends and family. She had just become an aunt and told her sister that she would baby-sit for her every Thursday night. Because she did *The Rules* and was not accepting last-minute dates from Matthew, she was able to stick to her commitment.

There was only one problem with the relationship. Matthew had still not proposed!

Lynn consulted with her sister, who suggested she have "a relationship talk" with him over a special candle-lit dinner. Lynn made Matthew's favorite dish, filet mignon with potatoes, but at the end of the meal, after complimenting her on how delicious dinner was, all he said was, "My parents' divorce was very traumatic. I'm just not ready for marriage. Why can't we just keep things the way they are?"

A friend of Lynn's suggested she buy him a book on "commitment-phobia" since Lynn was convinced that the fact that Matthew's parents divorced when he was only seven was one of the reasons he was gun-shy about marriage. Lynn bought him the book, and he said he would read it when he got a chance but never did and never brought it up again. Then Lynn suggested they talk to a marriage counselor to deal with his marriage jitters. He agreed but then found one excuse after another (late meeting, business presentation that needed last-minute preparation, basketball game, and so on). Lynn became increasingly impatient and started to question his commitment to their relationship on every date and in every phone conversation and e-mail. All Matthew ever said was "I love you. This is not a good time. Work is hectic."

Frustrated and hopeless, Lynn consulted us for advice. We told her to ask Matthew his intentions for the future once more, following the script in our "Closing the Deal" chapter in *The Rules II*. Again, Matthew said he wasn't ready, but could see getting married down the road. He refused to give a specific date or year. We told her that his answer was unacceptable, that after two years he either did or didn't want to marry her, that he already knew everything about her there was to know so it was a yes or a no at this point! Besides, we told her that at 35, she did not have another minute to waste with this man. We told her to tell him that she was "an old-fashioned girl and that she couldn't date him forever and that this relationship was not working out for her." We told her that she had to be on the No Contact plan from that moment on.

"What's No Contact?" Lynn asked, willing to do anything yet fearful of losing Matthew at the same time.

"No Contact means no dates, no calls, no e-mails; he can call and e-mail you and ask you out all he wants but you don't see him and you don't pick up the phone or call or e-mail him back until he says he's ready to get married," we told her. "And you don't tell him your strategy either, let him think you are busy or over him. Let him figure it out."

"But I love him and he loves me," she argued, "and we've been together for two years. How can I just stop everything cold turkey? And we have plans for the next few weeks, a concert, his cousin's wedding. . . . Isn't No Contact cruel?"

"If he doesn't love you enough to marry you, then he doesn't love you enough," we replied. "You've tried reasoning with him and candlelit dinners and other things, and nothing's worked. But you've never tried No Contact. Why not try it for 30 to 90 days and see what happens?" We explained that when a man still hasn't proposed after one and a half years of dating, No Contact is the only answer. If he can see you and speak to you without proposing, he has no incentive to marry you. Lynn said she understood and then got busy, too busy to see Matthew.

A week later Matthew e-mailed her, "Hi. How is your day going? Mine isn't going so great as I miss you." We told Lynn not to respond. A couple of days later, there was a phone call, "Hey, I was around the corner and thought I would stop by and say hi and pick up my umbrella. . . ." We told her not to call back or see him, but to mail him the umbrella with no note, which she did. A few more calls and e-mails followed but nothing worth responding to. Another week went by and Lynn was getting worried and called us. We said, "Sit tight and keep doing No Contact."

Sure enough, two weeks later Matthew e-mailed her a beautiful card which opened up into a ring and a smile. It said, "Can we meet for dinner to talk about us and our future?" She waited 24 hours and e-mailed back, "OK." He e-mailed back in five minutes, "How about tonight?"

It was Thursday and she baby-sat for her niece that night. She told him she couldn't as she "already had plans," but he knew what those plans were. While she was baby-sitting, the doorman buzzed, "Matthew is here."

He came up, got down on one knee, and said, "Look, I miss you and I realize that even though it's scary to get married and I have my fears about this, I want you and I want a baby like that too!" Her sister and brother-in-law came back early from their night out and they all had a glass of champagne (already iced) so it was a plan! She waited until the end of the evening and said "Yes, I'd love to."

Lynn realized that No Contact wasn't a cruel plan after all, but a way to get a man who loves you who may have issues to change his mind about marriage without pressuring or fighting with him. In the end, No Contact is as good for him (lets him come to his own decision, which men love to do) as it is for you (no hanging in there for years resentful that he is not proposing). When all else fails and everything's been said 100 times already, No Contact really works!

Rule 19

Keep Your Ad Up Until You Are Exclusive

Women take down their ads prematurely. They have two dates with a guy and think "He's the one, that's it for me, I don't want to meet anyone else," or they want to show Mr. Right on their third date that they are committed to him and him alone by taking down their ad. We think this is a big mistake. Regardless of the reason, we think the only time to take down your ad is when you are exclusive, he has said "I love you," or he has asked you to take down your ad—and he has taken his down too!

Jenna (WillowyBlond29) found this out the hard way. Mark (DreamGuy35) answered her ad and thought she was attractive and that they had a lot in common. Jenna flipped over his photo and profile (he was handsome and also loved the outdoors) and said "sure" when he asked her to meet for drinks in his second e-mail.

The first date on a Tuesday evening was perfect and ended with his asking her for dinner that Saturday night. Jenna was so crazy about Mark that she wouldn't even log onto the dating service under her own name that week, because it would have recorded her logging on and she didn't want Mark to think she was interested in meeting anyone else.

Like most women today, Jenna was so worried about men being commitment-phobic that she wanted to set an example of fidelity. She thought that if she showed a man that she was the exclusive type, he would follow in kind. Of course, this doesn't work. In fact, just the opposite is true, as Jenna soon discovered.

After a second date with Mark, a walk on the beach and a really great kiss, Jenna went home and took her ad down because she felt she had met the man she was going to marry. Taking her ad out of circulation was her way of proving to him that she was serious.

On their third date Mark mentioned that when he was searching through the ads to see her pretty photo again, he couldn't find it. She smiled sweetly and said that she took it down because she was so happy to have met him and did not want to meet anyone else. With that, Mark choked on his dinner. He said he wasn't feeling well and would she mind if they skipped dessert and coffee. And then he quickly dropped her off at her apartment building with just a peck on the cheek!

When Jenna didn't hear from Mark all week, she e-mailed him, "Everything OK?" He said, "Yes, just busy with work. Will call you when things settle down." When she didn't hear from him for another week, she called him at work and came right out and asked, "Are you dumping me?" Trying to be polite, he just said, "No, I just think we were moving a little too fast. I'm not looking for anything serious right now."

Jenna was speechless. She didn't understand what had happened until she consulted with us and we told her that taking down her ad and telling him about it (and why) was like asking a guy to marry you. "You can't ask a guy to be exclusive on the third date or any date. That's his job. Taking down your ad after the second date was premature, and *telling* him why you took it down was scary for him, which naturally made him lose interest," we explained. "Besides, Mark was not searching only for your photo that day but also for other women's photos. He's not ready to stop dating yet and neither should you be."

Jenna learned her lesson and put her ad back up. Mark saw it and e-mailed her for a date. This time, Jenna waited 48 hours and e-mailed him back, "Busy right now. Maybe next month." She waited until Mark e-mailed her again and again before she agreed to see him. Now she is dating him and three other guys she met online and loving it.

Jenna's new motto: "May the best man win!"

Rule 20

Don't Get Caught Up in Online Fantasy Relationships

In *The Rules II,* we told women that no matter what a man says, if he doesn't ask you out, the "relationship" is a fantasy—it's nothing. And nowhere are fantasy relationships more prevalent than on the Internet, where men can chat up a storm but never ask women out. Sadly, these women think they are in a relationship by the number of e-mails and Instant Messages they are getting from men, even though some of these men have never called nor met the women!

We understand that women sometimes want to lie to themselves, to dream. We understand that no matter how many times a woman has been hurt in love, mistreated, dumped, or divorced, she still wants to believe that there is someone special out there who will make it all up to her, maybe someone on love@aol or www.lavalife.com who will say and be all the things she wants. At least she hopes so. And if a man's e-mails sound like a BlueMountain.com card, which they often do online, she may already be planning the wedding.

Get a grip, girls! Don't succumb to a fantasy relationship with a man who's not dating you based on warm and fuzzy e-mails or Instant Message sessions, or you will surely get disappointed. Whatever you do, don't break up with your current boyfriend because you just got two e-mails from a sexy CEO with hazel green eyes or a bodybuilder who "loves your smile." You may never hear from Mr. CEO or Mr. Stud again (poof!), or you may hear from them but they may not ask for your number or ask you out.

So don't make major decisions based on winks and e-mail flirtations. Many of these don't pan out, so keep your feet on the ground until you have a couple of dates, at the very least, with someone.

"No, this really is the one!" you protest. "He read my profile and says we have so much in common. He's totally divorced, not separated. And I don't mind step-kids, really . . ."

We know how you feel. There is nothing more ego-boosting than the adoring e-mails of good-looking, not to mention rich, eligible bachelors. And when you are getting one, two, and three Instant Messages flashing on your screen at the same time from sweet-talking strangers, you think you are busy, that you have a lot going on in your love life at that moment, even though you will probably never meet any of them! Real life men pale beside the e-mails and Instant Messages of online men. E-mail men just know how to say the right thing. The truth is, they write whatever they have to in order to catch your interest so you e-mail them back. Why they are not this clever in person we don't know.

Here are some wonderful lines we have come across from men responding to women's ads:

> *"I love your eyes and smile. Let's take a spin in my new convertible and get to know each other better."*
> *"You are intoxicatingly beautiful. Would love to take you for a romantic Saturday night dinner. Hopefully you feel the same way about me."*
> *"I was going to quit online dating today . . . and then I saw your ad. Wow! Will you go out with me tonight, if not sooner? You won't be disappointed."*
> *"I noticed you are up very early [men want to show they are attentive and notice things about you and your ad] . . . would love to walk at dawn with you barefoot on the beach . . ."*
> *"I have everything I need in life, except the right woman to share it with . . . maybe you?"*
> *"Just saw your profile . . . I know this is destiny!"*
> *"I'm looking for my last first date!"*

Online men know exactly how to make women swoon and e-mail six girlfriends that they found Mr. Right in cyberspace. These men sprinkle their ads with stuff right out of Jackie Collins novels. One wrote, "I want a woman who appreciates sweet messages left on steamy bathroom mirrors and hugs for no occasion." By the way, this man poofed! right after he wrote all this—a form letter, no less.

In answer to the form questionnaire asking "Whom would you love to have lunch with?" one man wrote, "My future wife," and for future goals, he wrote, "I want to change my single status." If that didn't make the average woman faint, he also answered that his favorite movies were three weepy romances *When Harry Met Sally, Titanic,* and *Sleepless in Seattle.* You can see why some women start thinking about engagement rings after one e-mail!

Online men can suck you right in, especially when they throw in words like *wife, marriage, long-term commitment,* and *happily ever after.* This is like giving a woman a free shopping spree at Neiman Marcus. They all sound so enlightened, like men who have read relationship books; they're sincere, sweet, good listeners, and compassionate. Maybe they are sincere and all those other things, but maybe they are not. Time will tell.

The point is not to obsess over a man based on e-mails and a cute picture. Some guys just lay it on thick in their e-mails, prompting you to put your life on hold for them. You may even start fights with your real-life dates who don't seem to compare with your online fantasy guy. Don't! Keep your life and keep dating! If you are following all the online *Rules*—especially not e-mailing a man back who doesn't ask you out within four e-mails—you won't be able to lie to yourself about who is real and who isn't. Of course you can daydream and pin his photo on your bulletin board, but don't stop dating based on a fantasy relationship.

Rule 21

Never Date a Married Man, Even Online

There are women who have unknowingly met married men online. This can happen because there are men who routinely lie about their marital status online in order to conduct extramarital affairs—or even just flirtations. These women eventually find out (if they really want to) that these men are married, and, if they are smart, they stop seeing these guys.

It's hard to hide a marriage: Married men cannot give out their home numbers or go out every Saturday night, so they will eventually get caught by a real *Rules* girl. A non-*Rules* girl may not catch on because she will spontaneously accept a date on any night of the week. So if his wife goes shopping or has to work late, the married man can call a non-*Rules* girl and she will probably be available on a moment's notice. And because she has sex with him very quickly, she is reluctant to give him up even when she does find out he is married because she is already "involved."

A *Rules* girl is a whole different breed. She won't accept

spontaneous lunches and mid-week dates, especially if she is not being asked out for Saturday night. Everything has to be planned in advance and thus she may be just too much trouble for a married man to pursue.

This chapter is really for women who knowingly date men who are not even separated but still living with their wives under the same roof. We are talking about men who either answer an ad or send an Instant Message in a chat room: "Hi, beautiful . . . I'm in an unsatisfying marriage . . . I'm not happy, we sleep in separate rooms . . . I've already started looking at apartments . . ." We're talking about the women who believe these men and think they can get them, even though these men are most likely lying and are probably still sleeping with their wives. If you are dating a man who is still living in his house with his wife, kids, and dog, we say "Shame on you!"

Not only is it wrong and risky for you to date these men as they rarely marry the "other woman" or "the fun girl" or even the "transitional girl," but you are also making an enemy of his wife and kids, whom you will always have to deal with if you are lucky enough to get this guy down the road. So do it the right way and they won't hate you. Also, keep in mind that you may be shooting yourself in the foot with your affair as you are preventing yourself from being with truly available men. When you are obsessed with Mr. Married, you have less time and energy to give a fair shake to all the other single, separated, divorced, or widowed men who may be answering your ad or pursuing you offline.

So if you want to do things the proper and moral way and also increase your chances of getting Mr. Married to move out and date you, you should say, "Sorry, not interested. You can e-mail me when you're separated. Good luck!"

And then you must wait until he is out of his house—and we don't mean staying at his parents three times a week when he has a fight with his wife. He cannot just be looking at apartments, but have a lease for at least a year, a phone number, his own keys and toothbrush—and then he should be there for at least a few months! Obviously, you should not date a man who is out of his house for two days. You are only hurting yourself, because he could move back home in a jiffy and he is probably not ready for a serious relationship. Trust us—he is not jumping out of a marriage and committing so fast to you. And buyer beware with a man who goes back and forth with his wife. Sometimes a man will be out of his house when you meet him and then move back in or you find out he is seeing his wife and he tells you he still has feelings for her, or his kids are crying, or one of them needs surgery. If that is the case, the rule is: The second he moves back in or starts seeing his wife is the second you stop seeing him. And think about it: Do you really want or need a man like this in your life?

Do not try to cheat the system. Do not think, "If I date him while he still sees his wife and cook, clean, or shop for him, maybe he'll pick me over her," or worse, "It's OK for him to live with his wife while we date, why upset the kids?" and "Why should he waste money on an apartment?" or "Why jeopardize his mother-in-law's inheritance, which he gets half of? That way *we'll* have more money when he finally does move out and we are together!" These strategies rarely work because they are sleazy and filled with bad motives.

Heather (BuxomBeauty44), found this out the hard way. Barry (HotLawyer49) answered her ad, which consisted of several photos in *Playboy*-type poses and come-hitherish writing (for example, her hobbies included "sitting in a hot tub with a sexy guy"). Need we say it? This is non-*Rules* behavior (see *Rules 3, 4,* and *5*). She figured she would compensate for being 30 pounds overweight by baring her cleavage.

In his first e-mail to Heather around midnight on a weeknight after his wife went to bed, Barry told her that her photos left him speechless. But he also came right out and said he and his wife were still living together but that the relationship was just on paper, that they didn't sleep together, and he was going to be leaving soon but couldn't right now because of finances and three kids. He told her he knew it wasn't a great situation for a single woman to get into, but she should give him a chance. "Let's e-mail or Instant Message each other a little bit," he said, "and see where it might lead. You never know . . ."

In his photo, he was incredibly handsome with big blue eyes, and Heather found him irresistible. Rather than do *The Rules* and say, "Thanks, but no thanks. E-mail me when you are separated and good luck with your marriage," Heather Instant Messaged him the next night around 7 P.M.: "Thanks for your honesty. Sorry to hear about your marriage, how long are you married and why are you so unhappy?" Usually, Barry couldn't talk at that hour, but his wife was working late. He immediately shot back an Instant Message to Heather.

This is the Instant Message exchange that ensued:

HotLawyer49: *Married 18 years. We started dating in college. I thought she was nice, we became good friends and then I kind of grew to love her because she was always there for me . . . So two years after college, I thought to myself she would make a good wife and I proposed. She's solid, but I'm bored. There's no sex, no passion, just chores and errands and birthday parties for the kids and soccer practice and*

*doubling with other couples on Saturday night. I need more
excitement than that . . .*

BuxomBeauty44: *Does your wife know how you feel?*

HotLawyer49: *More or less . . . Last year, I had a three-month
affair with a woman I work with and she found out and
was devastated, but she forgave me when I broke it off. . . .
But I think she knows that I'm not happy . . .*

BuxomBeauty44: *So why aren't you moving out sooner?*

HotLawyer49: *The kids. Money. I don't have the money right
now for my own place, I'm paying for braces and camp for
three kids . . . so I have to worry about that . . . What about
you? Why is such a beautiful and sexy woman like you still
single?*

BuxomBeauty44: *Thanks. Well, I just gained 30 pounds after
a bad breakup. I've been engaged twice. It's hard to find a
good man . . . someone who would be faithful and take care
of me.*

HotLawyer49: *Well, I think you look unbelievably hot even
with the 30 pounds! I'd certainly have no reason to cheat if I
were with you, that's for sure . . . you could be a model. How
about we continue this over a drink or dinner? It's getting
late and I have an early morning meeting tomorrow . . .*

BuxomBeauty44: *Well, I don't usually do this but you seem so
sincere . . .*

HotLawyer49: *Great! Why don't we meet for lunch near your
office tomorrow? What's the best way to reach you?*

BuxomBeauty44: *OK. I guess there's no harm in meeting just
once. My cell # is 555-5515. I leave it on all the time.*

Barry called later that night and they met for lunch the next
day (when a woman dates a married man, as we said, she doesn't

usually stick to the no-last-minute-date *Rule)* where they split a bottle of wine and made out in a dark booth in the back of the restaurant.

Heather got back to her office, a little tipsy and definitely intoxicated with HotLawyer49. She e-mailed him right away, "Thanks for lunch, it was delicious!" and signed it with a happy face.

They e-mailed and Instant Messaged each other every night after midnight after Barry's wife went to bed. The online relationship was perfect for him: no phone calls, no evidence. His wife thought he was on the computer every night working on a big case. Meanwhile, the e-mails got steamier and steamier and Barry started forwarding them to a couple of his friends and bragging about his new busty blond girlfriend.

On their fourth lunch date Barry suggested they skip the restaurant altogether and go to a hotel where they had sex three times and ordered from room service. Heather was convinced that Barry was falling in love with her because he wanted to see her every week. He would either ask her to meet him for lunch or at a hotel and he even sent a dozen roses to her office for no special occasion and signed the card XOXO. He was so gorgeous and so good in bed that she didn't mind that all he talked about were his problems (wife, kids, money, work), that he never asked about her, and that he didn't bring up moving out of his house anymore. She was just so happy to be with him on any level. She ignored all the other responses to her ad and eventually took her ad down because she didn't want Barry to get jealous or to think she was not committed to him. Besides, she was sure that Barry would be leaving his wife soon.

After three months, Barry started to complain about the expense of meeting at a hotel and ordering three-course meals with champagne from room service. He wondered since she lived so close to her office if she wouldn't mind meeting in her apartment and fixing tuna sandwiches with potato chips and Coke—not Pepsi, he liked Coke, he told her.

Heather didn't mind at all. She thought it was wife-y to make him lunch and figured they would live in her apartment as soon as he moved out of his house to save money, so why not get used to it now. This was because Heather thought she could beat the system and get a married man.

But after six months and still no moving-out talk, Heather was getting fed up with sandwiches and sex in her apartment and decided to drop hints in her e-mails about their future. When that didn't work, she decided to bring it up in person, over lunch and even during sex. Barry's answer was always the same, "I'm not ready and I told you there were no guarantees when we got into this . . . right now, I can't give you more than this," and finally one day he said, "If you want more, you're going to have to find someone else."

Heather ignored what he said and continued to pressure Barry to move out and to be with her more often until he moved out. For example, she begged him to come to her office Christmas party on a weeknight (even though Barry's rule was "Just lunch, no nights") and to go away with her for a weekend and make up some excuse to tell his wife. Barry's answer was always no. Fed up, Heather finally asked him, "You say you love me, but are you really planning to leave your wife . . . or is this just about sex?"

Cornered, Barry finally confessed that he was not in love with Heather and that he would probably not leave his wife because she was a good woman and the mother of his children and he would never do anything to hurt her again. "We can still meet for lunch, but I'm off the screen for anything else," he told her. When she screamed at him that he had led her on, Barry decided to end the relationship right then and there and told her never to e-mail him again. He even changed his e-mail address!

Heather was heartbroken.

In fact, two months later, while Barry was having lunch with his wife at a restaurant near his office, Heather walked in with a girlfriend and Barry didn't even say hello or look in her direction. He didn't even excuse himself to go to the bathroom so he could swing by and say a quick hello. He just looked down at his plate the whole time and pretended not to see her. He then got the check as soon as he could and left with his arm around his wife.

Heather was so devastated that she couldn't eat lunch and cried so much that her eye makeup ran all over her face. She was too upset to go back to work and even called in sick the next day. It took her six months to get over Barry.

Heather called us for a consultation and we told her that cheating the system never works and to stay away from married men for good. We suggested she go on a diet and go back online but change her screen name to "BlondBeauty" and post a nice smiling headshot and take out the reclining Playboy-type photos. We also told her to take out the suggestive comments about "sitting in a hot tub with a sexy guy" and put in her hobbies, which were "tennis and swing dancing."

Heather took our advice and swore she had learned her lesson, having lost not only her self-esteem and self-respect, but a year of her life, a year that could have been spent dating Mr. Right.

Why find out the hard way? Learn from Heather and countless other women who dated married men and paid the price. Don't make the same mistake! Never date a married man—ever!

Rule 22

Don't Ruin Your Real-Life Relationship over an Online Flirtation

It used to be that what broke up relationships and marriages were men and women having affairs with busty secretaries, friendly stewardesses, understanding coworkers, and handsome bosses. Today, online flirtations that move to real life are also destroying relationships. We have heard about both men and women, perhaps a little unhappy or bored with their partners, cruising chat rooms and making pen pals who may or may not then become their lovers. Their real-life partners find out and the damage can be devastating.

So buyer beware! Online flirtations are not harmless. Unless you are willing to lose your existing relationship, think twice before wandering into chat rooms. Men will Instant Message you, ask you about the posted chat-room topic, and you don't know how far that will go. They may end up asking you whether you would like to "continue chatting over coffee or lunch." And if you are feeling ignored or if you just had a fight with your significant other, this may seem like a good idea.

Here are two sad stories of online flirtations that destroyed good real-life relationships.

Jennifer, 29, a third-grade schoolteacher, who was dating Peter, 33, an M.B.A., for almost a year, felt she had found her soul mate in this good-looking, kind, and caring businessman. In fact, they had talked about getting engaged and were planning to go ring shopping after he got back from a week-long business trip to London. Peter was logging in mega-hours on nights and weekends for a big merger. Jennifer was happy that she was marrying someone so hard-working, but at the same time, she felt a little lonely. She was used to spending every weekend with Peter. Meanwhile, her three closest friends were busy dating and two of them were meeting guys in singles chat rooms. They were constantly e-mailing her about their dates and forwarding her men's profiles to check out and it seemed as if they were having all the fun!

One evening, Peter called from London to say that there were problems with the deal he was doing and that he wouldn't be back for another week. Bored and not sure what to do that night, Jennifer went online and made up a screen name, SchoolTeacher2. She decided that if anyone Instant Messaged her she would call herself "Beth" just to be safe. She clicked into the local singles chat room her friends had told her so much about. It seemed like everyone knew each other and she didn't know what to say. She was about to log off when CoolGuy31 Instant Messaged her.

"Hi. I'm Oz. That's my code name. My favorite movie is *The Wizard of Oz*. I'm going for my master's in special education. Who are you? Are you a teacher? What kind?"

Jennifer Instant Messaged him back: "Hi, my name is Beth. I teach third grade."

They chatted about what made them go into teaching (love kids, summers off) and realized how much they had in common, including tennis and hiking. Oz was funny as well, telling her jokes and hysterical stories about online dates he had been on where the women were so unattractive (sometimes their photos were 10 years old) that he didn't even want to finish his drink. He even told her about his "code" with his best friend whereby he would call Oz on his cell within the first 10 minutes of a date so Oz could make up an excuse to leave a bad date.

During the entire conversation, Jennifer was thinking how Peter was her soul mate but that, as of late, he'd been very serious and businesslike because of his extra workload, while Oz seemed so much fun to talk to. He was better than anything on TV! So after an hour of Instant Messaging each other, Oz asked Beth if she wanted to meet sometime for coffee to continue their chat.

"No thanks. I'm involved with someone and it's serious," she replied.

"Then what are you doing in a singles chat room?" he asked.

"My boyfriend is on a business trip and my friends are into this so I just wanted to check it out," she replied.

Soon Jennifer became addicted, logging on every night to see what Oz had to say. The second she got on, Oz would Instant Message her, "Another bad date . . . she was like 40 pounds overweight and didn't stop talking except to put another forkful of food in her mouth! I got the check and ran out. Sometimes I wish you were available, you seem really nice and easy to be with. Are you sure we can't just meet for a quick drink?" Beth (Jennifer) would always answer, "I'd love to but I can't . . ."

Three weeks later Peter went on another business trip. They still hadn't gone ring shopping because he wanted to wait until he got his bonus. Jennifer felt lonely again so that night she logged on to chat with Oz.

Once again he asked her for coffee.

This time, she thought, "Why not? There's no harm, it's totally platonic. Peter's away anyway. We'll laugh for an hour and I'll go home."

When she got to the coffee place, she saw one of Peter's basketball buddies who she thought was totally obnoxious. "Hey, Mark, what are you doing here?"

"I'm meeting this girl I met online, she's supposed to be hot. What are you doing here?"

"I'm just meeting a girlfriend," she lied.

"Where's Peter?" he asked.

"On another business trip," she replied.

They stared at each other for about 20 minutes. Finally Mark said, "Oh my God, you must be Beth! She said she would be wearing a pink sweater! I'm Oz."

Jennifer was so startled, she didn't even think to lie. "I can't believe it's you! Listen, whatever you do, please don't tell Peter . . . I wasn't looking to meet anyone. All my friends are meeting guys online and I just wanted to check it out. We're going ring shopping when he gets back from LA. Please don't say anything! Let's just keep this between you and me, OK?" she pleaded.

"Peter's a good friend of mine, I have to say something. You shouldn't be in singles chat rooms. He doesn't deserve this.

How do I know I'm the only guy? Maybe you have a couple of online boyfriends you see when Peter is away. . . ."

"You're crazy. I don't have any boyfriends and I haven't done anything wrong. You're a creep if you say anything! Good-bye!" she told him and ran out.

Mark called Peter the second he came back to town and told him the story. Peter called Jennifer and went ballistic. "I've been working day and night like a dog and you're cruising chat rooms and going on dates with men? It's a good thing I didn't buy you a ring. We're over!" he told her.

Jennifer tried to tell him it was all very innocent, but Peter said he couldn't trust her and ended their relationship two days before their one-year anniversary. Jennifer was devastated.

If you don't want what happened to Jennifer to happen to you, don't cruise online if you are in a good real-life relationship. If you are in a chat room because of an interest in politics or skiing or something, keep to the subject and don't get personal with anyone and definitely don't meet them in real life. Once you make the move from an online flirtation to a real-life meeting, you are on the proverbial slippery slope toward cheating.

Sarah's situation was even more serious than Jennifer's. She lost a three-year marriage to Bob. The couple, both 40, had met on a blind date and hit it off. They both loved dancing and going out to dinner and shows. They were best friends. For Sarah, the only thing missing was that Bob did not share her enthusiasm for politics. A diehard Republican, Sarah worked as an assistant to a political consultant, was addicted to news shows, and read three newspapers a day. Bob, a dentist and sports junkie, couldn't care less about politics and didn't even vote in the last election. Sarah wished she could talk to Bob about her passion for politics, but having tried for three years, she finally gave up. So one weekend when Bob was at a dental convention, Sarah went into a political chat room. She found it to be quite stimulating. Several men Instant Messaged her and she loved the camaraderie and intellectual banter.

Soon Sarah became addicted. At night, after Bob went to sleep, she put her bathrobe on and tiptoed into the den to log on to her computer. This went on for weeks and weeks. She didn't say anything to Bob because the chat room was made up mostly of men and she didn't want him to think she was doing anything wrong.

One night, Jim (HandsomeEngineer49) Instant Messaged Sarah and they chatted for two hours about the election, the national budget, the problem with the Democratic Party, and eventually their personal lives. He was an engineer with his own firm and a staunch Republican, recently divorced with two teenage daughters. Every night Sarah couldn't wait until Bob went to bed so she could Instant Message Jim. Eventually Jim asked if they could talk on the phone and Sarah gave him her work number.

One day Jim called her at work and said, "I'm in your neighborhood, can I buy you lunch?" Sarah thought it was harmless enough. They met, sipped piña coladas, and two hours later Sarah went back to work completely infatuated with Jim's intellect. He was brilliant and fascinating to talk to.

They started to meet for lunch, first once a week, then twice a week. There were phone calls every day in the office and e-mails and Instant Messages at night. The more she and Jim spoke and Instant Messaged each other, the more boring Bob became. Jim was exciting, suave, witty, and, most important, a Republican like Sarah who also voted for George W. Bush. Jim was also passionate about politics, which Sarah found fascinating. Bob was solid and trustworthy, but some-times she felt all he could talk about was his new teeth-whitening system and baseball. Sarah felt a little guilty, but since she and Jim had not kissed or even held hands, she did not think she was cheating. Besides, she felt that it was all very innocent since Bob wasn't interested in politics and wasn't the jealous type either.

Then one afternoon during lunch and a few glasses of wine, Jim leaned over and said, "I think you have some tomato sauce on your cheek . . ." and kissed her on her cheek. Just when Sarah was about to say, "Please don't do that," Jim kissed her on the lips and thus began a steamy two-month extramarital affair. Although this was never her intention—she'd only been looking for someone to talk politics with—Sarah had to admit she was smitten.

One night, Bob woke up around midnight to get a glass of water and noticed the light coming out of the den. Sarah had gone into the bathroom in the middle of an Instant Message chat with Jim and left her computer on.

Bob could read the steamy Instant Messages and refer-ences to "lunch at our table tomorrow" between his wife and HandsomeEngineer49. He was flabbergasted and confronted her.

First Sarah denied everything, explaining that she met him in a chat room but never in person and that it was nothing. But Bob did not believe it. The next morning he figured out her password—it was the same as her bank password—and read all the incriminating e-mails. He called his best friend, met with an attorney, and filed for divorce. That night, he packed his bags and moved out. Sarah tried to talk to Bob as he collected his things, but he wouldn't listen.

Once she realized that her marriage was really over, she thought "Maybe this was meant to be, maybe I am meant to be with Jim." She called Jim and told him what happened, thinking he would be happy to hear that they didn't have to sneak around anymore and they could see each other on Saturday nights. She told him she couldn't wait to meet him for lunch the next day.

When Jim didn't call her for lunch, she called him. He said he was in the middle of a meeting and would have to talk to her later.

When he didn't call later either, Sarah tried him at home. No answer. She went online that night and he wasn't there. She called him at work the next day and he said, "Look, I'm sorry about what happened, but I never intended to break up a marriage. I'm just out of a long relationship myself and I'm not looking for anything serious. I think you're pretty, nice, and smart, but I don't want more than the relationship we have, you know lunch and . . . you know what I mean. Anyway, I have to go, I have a client coming in five minutes. . . ."

"You mean you don't want to see me this weekend? I thought we could be together now. Like a real couple."

"Look, I don't want more than what we have. Why don't you try to work things out with your husband? I'm afraid we don't want the same things . . . anyway, I have to go, my client is here. If you want to meet for lunch sometime, call me."

Sarah couldn't believe it. It felt like a bad dream, a nightmare. Only a few weeks ago she had a husband and a pretty good marriage, but because of something that started as a silly online flirtation, she lost her husband and then her online Casanova a day later! She was all alone. How did this happen? How could a chat room relationship wreak such havoc? This was earth-shattering. She had so many pieces of her life to make sense of. She didn't know where to begin . . .

Of course, no one thinks such a thing can happen to them, but it does, every day. So buyer beware. No matter how tempted you are, don't sacrifice a real-life relationship for an online flirtation because you're bored for five minutes. It could go from being a dream to a nightmare and then end up leaving you all alone with remorse and self-loathing.

If you do have an online buddy for some good, innocent reason, handle it like Brittany, who liked to go into a backgammon chat room on those nights when she didn't have a date with her boyfriend, Scott, whom she had been seeing for about a year.

A few times Scott called and could tell her mind was elsewhere. "What are you doing?" he asked. "Work," she lied. She wasn't sure how he would react to her having online male buddies.

But when he asked Brittany the same question again during a phone conversation a few weeks later, she decided that she couldn't lie anymore and since what she was doing was completely innocent, how could he think she was cheating?

"You know how crazy I am about backgammon? Well, believe it or not, there's this backgammon chat room that I go into a few times a week. It's really fun," she told him.

"Hey, I've heard about chat rooms. Aren't they really for men to hit on women?" he asked.

"No, this isn't a singles chat room, this is strictly about the topic, backgammon. Really," she replied.

"Yeah, right!" he said.

"I'm telling you the truth," she insisted.

"I don't know about this, I just hope you're not e-mailing any men. Stick to the women, OK?" he said.

"Well, actually I've made both male and female buddies, but they're really cool and funny. There's this guy BackgammonKing34 who is hysterical. He's a real character, I think you would like him. Why don't you come over and see for yourself?" she said.

The next night Scott stopped by, went into the chat room with Brittany and decided to have some fun with it.

He Instant Messaged BackgammonKing34 "Hey, Backgammon King, I know you have no interest in backgammon and you're just trying to pick up women. Just leave my girlfriend alone, OK?"

BackgammonKing34: "Don't worry. I have a girlfriend. I've been into backgammon since college."

Scott e-mailed him back: "Cool."

They both laughed and continued to chat with a few of her backgammon buddies for the rest of the night.

Brittany was glad she told Scott about it. She knew if he found out by accident, he would be upset and maybe not trust her. And being honest about it worked in her favor. Every time Scott came over they went into the chat room together. It became part of their Sunday night ritual, along with ordering in sushi and watching *Sex and the City.*

The moral of the story is, if you do have an online buddy of the opposite sex, keep it to the computer, don't meet him in person, and do tell your significant other about your online buddy. Or, like Jennifer and Sarah, you could lose your real-life relationship.

Rule 23

Don't Be Jealous of Non-*Rules* Girls Online

To recap: If you are doing *The Rules,* you are not answering men's ads. You are not Instant Messaging them. You are not responding to their e-mails in a few hours, much less minutes or seconds. Your e-mails are factual, short, and polite, not romantic or racy. You are weeding out time-wasters, angry men, and other undesirables, so maybe only 25 of every 100 responses you get are real contenders.

Your non-*Rules* friends, on the other hand, are answering ads, Instant Messaging men in chat rooms, e-mailing men back right away, and writing up a storm, so more e-mails are being exchanged. They are busier than you, they have more online relationships, possibly more dates, and seemingly more fun. They are meeting men on a dime for coffee, picking up strange men at airports, or flying out to meet them. You are only mildly busy. It takes about an hour a day for you to read your mail and e-mail men back, and then you go back to your regular life, whereas your non-*Rules* friends have made online dating their whole life. They are practically glued to their computers. They are living a constant online soap opera.

In between Instant Messaging men, they are also Instant Messaging you and five other girlfriends about the state of their relationships. There is so much commotion going on that you have to admit you are a little jealous. Breaking *The Rules* seems so much more exciting than counting the hours (24 to be exact) before you answer men's e-mails. You probably think you are either doing something wrong, or else you think you are doing something right but it is soooooo boring. You want to be *bad*. You may even question *The Rules* and wonder why you have to be so good.

We know how you feel. Most *Rules* girls have felt this way from time to time, especially at parties where non-*Rules* girls are talking to, and dancing with, the cutest guys in the room because these women aggressively approached the guys first. At times like that, a *Rules* girl can feel as if she's standing on a line for an hour to get into a hot new club and watching people sneak in ahead of her. Not fair!

When non-*Rules* girls start online relationships by making the first e-mail move, they are essentially cutting in line, trying to cheat or bypass the natural order of things. The natural order of things is that man pursues woman. When a non-*Rules* girl Instant Messages a man or asks him out, she is not trusting that there is a Mr. Right out there for her who will eventually contact her online or in real life. She either doesn't believe or can't wait and acts desperately. She has to make it happen. It is all about fear and low self-esteem.

But we assure you that the grass is not always greener on the other side. If you hang in there, you will find that *The Rules* work in the long run, although it may not be so much fun in the short run. Keep your eyes on your own plate—and on the prize, which will be a man who seeks you out and wants you and only you! Yes, you are on the slow plan, but it's the old tortoise and hare story. You will triumph in the end.

Right now, your non-*Rules* friends have quantity and busyness, but not quality. They may have five wild online relationships, while you are waiting for one nice guy to answer your ad. Non-*Rules* girls get everything quickly, but these relationships fade as fast as they get started, so don't be jealous.

Julie (PrettyBlond29) is a true-blue *Rules* girl. She reads the books regularly, even highlights them, and she doesn't make a move without first consulting us or a *Rules* contact. She got 65 responses to her ad, weeded them down to 15, and met 12 over a period of three months. She spent about an hour a day checking her mail and waited 24 hours to answer e-mails. Occasionally she'd venture into a chat room such as ThirtiesLove and respond when men Instant Messaged her, but she kept it short.

She met one man this way. His Instant Message said, "Hi, so what's a pretty blond like you doing in a place like this? LOL" and he was very polite and professional and she agreed to meet him for a date zero. Julie met him for drinks one night after work and liked him enough to date him for two months, but ended the relationship before they slept together when she realized she wasn't in love with him. From time to time, Julie would venture into singles chat rooms, where men would Instant Message her. If no one Instant Messaged her, she would log off. If they Instant Messaged her "A.S.L." (Age, Sex, Location), she ignored them and called it a night.

Meanwhile, Julie's non-*Rules* friend Rhonda (WildNFun32)

was on the computer all day, e-mailing and Instant Messaging men and living in singles chat rooms. She met 20 men and slept with half of them. Although none of these relationships lasted more than a few weeks, she was busier than Julie. She was throwing lingerie in and out of suitcases. She flew to Martha's Vineyard to meet a rich divorced guy for a weekend, she met a European jet-setter for drinks at a hot spot the next day, and her cell phone was ringing off the hook. While Rhonda was ordering lacy things from Victoria's Secret, Julie was in sweats counting down the 24 hours before e-mailing two men back and counting their e-mails to see if they had asked for her phone number by their fourth e-mail. So much for fun, Julie thought. Is this fair?

But Julie hung in there and believed in *The Rules,* and she eventually watched Rhonda's non-*Rules* relationships unravel and realized she was doing the right thing. Rhonda called from Martha's Vineyard to say that the rich, divorced guy wasn't as good-looking or smart as she previously thought. The next day she called to complain that the European jet-setter confessed that he was only separated from his wife, not divorced, and that they still slept together occasionally. That did not stop her from having sex with him and wanting to see him again. She thought he felt the same way or so he said, but when she e-mailed him a few days later, it came back undelivered. He had changed his e-mail address! Rhonda was totally embarrassed but she decided to get over him by Instant Messaging a new guy in a chat room 10 minutes later.

So things are not so wonderful for non-*Rules* girls, but rather than learn from their experiences, they continue to break *Rules,* thinking, "This time will be different." On the other hand, Julie and you (hopefully) are farther along than you think, even though you are not meeting as many men and have no wild experiences to send to *Cosmo.*

By doing *The Rules,* you are learning to trust that the right man will find your ad, think "wow," and e-mail you. And you will have a *Rules* relationship that lasts longer than a weekend on Martha's Vineyard!

Journal Your Online Dating Experiences

Before we published *The Rules Dating Journal,* a diary for dating behavior, in 1997, many women we did consultations with had this "terminal vagueness" or amnesia about dating. They couldn't remember how the relationship started or what *Rules* they did or didn't do.

When we asked them simple questions: "Who spoke to whom first?" "Who called whom?" "How long did you speak on the phone?" " How often did you see each other?" "Who brought up exclusivity?" each time they drew a blank.

We are now seeing a lot of this self-defeating terminal-vagueness behavior online. Why? Because the very nature of online dating lends itself to fantasy and vagueness. Scores of women have told us that they are on the computer every day e-mailing and Instant Messaging men, losing track of time and losing the guys as well. For some women, online dating is like a drug, a surreal world, where time and *Rules* seemingly do not exist.

For example, Sandy, a pretty, 33-year-old bookkeeper who never bounced a check in her life and was meticulous about buying birthday presents and taking her car to be serviced on time, could not answer the most basic questions about her relationship during our phone consultation. These are Sandy's answers:

> I have no idea, honestly, I really don't know . . . everything was kind of mutual, we met in a ThirtiesLove chat room, or maybe a FortiesLove chat room, I don't remember, I had four screens going on at once; I don't remember if he Instant Messaged me first or I Instant Messaged him, we exchanged numbers and he called me and left a message and then I called him back; we spoke for 20 minutes the first time, no, maybe an hour; he asked me out for drinks, then I asked him out for the second date, I had two tickets to a baseball game; we didn't exactly have dates after that, we just hung out a lot. We Instant Messaged every day quite a bit. In April we went to Europe for five days, his idea, he had a business trip and brought me along, but then he had to cut it short. After that it was sort of mutual, him e-mailing and Instant Messaging me and me doing the same, there was no real pursuer. I can't remember anything else. This is really hard.

Online or not, dating this way is a big mistake.

When women like Sandy ask us, "How am I supposed to remember everything?," we say, "Just write down every *Rule* you are doing and not doing." When they did what we said, they reported back that they became more aware of what was going on in their relationships and broke fewer *Rules*. Journaling works!

A *Rules* dating journal is not to be confused with a journal that encourages you to record men's names, professions, hobbies, favorite color, favorite cologne, birth date, names of their kids, events in their life, and so on, so that when men Instant Message you or e-mail you or call you, you have handy conversation material at your fingertips and can show them how interested you are in them. No, obsessing on these details has nothing to do with *The Rules Dating Journal,* whose sole purpose is to help you see and correct self-defeating dating behavior.

You know how you make a "to do" list so you don't forget to do errands, or how you write down your expenses when you decide it's time to budget, or how you count calories in a notebook when you are going on a serious diet? Well, the same applies to online dating. Writing down your online dating experiences will raise your consciousness and help you change your behavior. Journaling will prevent you from being dumb or sloppy about your online habits. We suggest you journal every day (or every week, whatever works for you) for 10 minutes so that you are less likely to break *Rules* online.

Below are 25 questions we suggest you answer for each online relationship you are in and then share it with a close friend or a therapist or a *Rules* buddy. No need to write your autobiography or an essay. Just get the facts down and you will see results. For one thing, it will be harder to lie to yourself or be in a fog when you see your mistakes in black and white. And it will be easier to do *The Rules* when you have written down your online activity. Of course, the best time to write in your journal is when you want to break a *Rule* such as answer a man's ad or e-mail a man back too soon!

1. Before reading *The Rules for Online Dating,* how did you date online? Did you have any specific *Rules* of your own?

2. What problems are you experiencing online, such as men e-mailing or Instant Messaging a lot but not asking you out?

3. What are your personal weaknesses (unable to resist answering men's ads, not realizing that this is the same as asking a man out)?

4. What online dating *Rules* are you committed to following today or this week?

5. If you are currently in a relationship where you met online:

- Who e-mailed or Instant Messaged whom first?
- Did he answer your ad, did you answer his ad, or did you meet in a chat room?
- In general, who e-mails whom first and more often or Instant Messages whom first, and who ends Instant Message sessions first?

6. If you initially met in person but are now calling or e-mailing each other in between dates, who is initiating calls or e-mails?

7. Are your e-mails short (three sentences) or long (a page)?

8. Are you sending smiley faces :), coffee cups, flowers or greeting cards, friendship thoughts, and songs for no occasion because you think they're cute? Or are you really sending them to remind him you exist? (Not good.)

9. Are you waiting at least 24 hours to e-mail him back? (Good.)

10. Are you allowing him to Instant Message you all day long? (Not good.)

11. Are you being careful to:

• not use your real name as your screen name(s)?

• block yourself so he can't Instant Message you, or just not respond to his IMs, or say you are too busy to chat? (Good.)

12. Who initially suggested moving from e-mail to phone?

13. Who initially suggested meeting in person?

14. Did he contact you after the first date by e-mail or phone? (Good.) Or is he just using Instant Messaging to catch you online? (Not good.)

15. Are you having regular dates with e-mails and phone calls in between? (Good.) Or is it basically an e-mail relationship with few or no dates because he always has a good excuse like he's busy with work or out of town, one of his parents is sick, or he has his kids for the next five weekends? (Not good.)

16. How long have you been dating? Has he said he wants to be exclusive or asked you to take down your ad?

17. Has he said "I love you" (ILY)?

18. If it's been more than four months since you met, do you feel like you are in a relationship? Or are you constantly asking your girlfriends what they think and feeling insecure and not knowing what is going on between you and him?

19. Is he e-mailing you or calling you in advance (Wednesday for Saturday night) for a date? (Good.) Or is he just catching you when he can in an Instant Message online and asking you for last-minute dates because he doesn't plan in advance for whatever reason? (Not good.)

20. Is his ad still up even though he denies it? And when you ask him about it; does he say, "Oh, it is? I forgot to take it down," and then you still see it up? Does this make you feel crazy? (Not good.)

21. Have you caught him in singles-oriented chat rooms or found him listed on other dating sites?

22. Has he involved you in his life? Have you doubled with his friends, gone to a party with him, or met his parents? Have you involved him in your life, your parties, your friends?

23. If this is a long-distance relationship, has he visited you? Or has he visited you once and now that you are hooked on him, does he expect you to visit him all the time because he claims he can't get away (business, kids, etc.)?

24. Or has he said nothing about visiting you, or you visiting him, because although he says he wants a relationship all he really wants to be is pen pals?

25. What is your success rate with answering men's ads versus letting men answer your ad?

26. If you could redo an online relationship that went wrong, what would you do differently?

On a daily or weekly basis you should answer the following 10 questions:

1. Are you following *The Rules* in your online behavior? If so, which ones?

2. If not, what *Rules* are you breaking? Answering men's ads? Letting men waste your time with endless Instant Message sessions without asking you out?

3. Is your ad light and breezy?

4. Are your answers to essay questions as short as possible?

5. Have you shortened your answers since reading this book?

6. Have you taken out anything about your past relationships and deleted anything about your demands and aspirations for your next relationship?

7. Have you taken out your income (nobody's business)?

8. Is your photo recent and flattering? Are you smiling?

9. Is your ad upbeat and your essay answers not too therapy oriented?

10. Are you in a real relationship with this man you met online? (Good.) Or are you merely his date for weddings and trips? (Not good.)

Be honest! The truth will set you free for a healthy relationship.

Don't Break or Bend *The Rules* Online—Even a Little Bit

Nothing good happens when you bend *The Rules* even a little bit, in person or online, as we have outlined for you in this book. Any *Rule*-bending behavior eventually shows up in your relationship.

Here are some true stories of what can happen when *The Rules* are broken:

Joanne, 37, a headhunter with big almond eyes, a corner office at a big recruiting firm, and her own condo, couldn't wait until this book came out, so she booked a consultation with us last year to find out exactly what the Internet *Rules* are. We helped her write her ad (ExoticBeauty37), select a smiling headshot, and told her not to answer men's ads, but to let them answer hers. Her ad generated more than 200 responses, which she whittled down to 20 after screening out men who were either too young or just not her type. Just about every e-mail she got was complimentary and flirtatious, but few asked for her telephone number or to meet.

Frantically, she contacted us wanting to know what to do. We told her that if a man didn't ask for her number or ask to meet her within four e-mails, it was "next!" and to stop e-mailing him back. Joanne admitted that she thought our advice was too strict but promised to try to follow it. Putting a four-e-mail limit to date zero was easy to do with the men she wasn't interested in. But when InvestmentBanker45 answered her ad, *The Rules* went out the window!

His first e-mail to her was: "Wow! Hello gorgeous! I turned on my computer this morning and your smile woke me up! You really are a beauty! I'm divorced with a son and a stepson. I have everything I want—a nice home, a luxury car and a boat—but I am missing that special someone. . . . Tell me more about you!"

Joanne was thrilled because InvestmentBanker45 lived nearby, just in the next town. She waited 24 hours to respond and, trying to do *The Rules*, e-mailed back, "I'm a headhunter, recently divorced, no kids. I love to dance, ski, travel . . ."

Investment Banker45's second e-mail was: "I love to ski too. . . . Are you looking just to date or for something more serious?"

Oh, no, she thought, a trick question! Joanne consulted with us about this one and we told her something she did not want to hear: "It's not good when they ask you what you are looking for, but with no date question in sight!"

Joanne decided to e-mail him back a "non-answer" answer: "Gosh, I'll have to think about that one."

Investment Banker45's third e-mail was: "What happened with your marriage? What did you learn? I've learned lots of lessons from my marriage, like communication is the key, and I don't want to make the same mistakes again."

Oh, no, she thought, another tricky question! We told Joanne we didn't like it, too many questions from someone you've never met and still no questions about meeting.

Joanne decided to respond with, "We just grew apart. Yes, I think it's good to learn from past relationships. I've learned a lot too."

Joanne was praying that he would ask for her number or suggest meeting in his next (fourth) e-mail and make it a *Rules* relationship. But Investment Banker45's fourth e-mail was: "How long are you divorced? Have you been dating a lot online?"

Joanne's heart sank. But rather than consult us this time, she told herself that the fourth e-mail Rule was totally arbitrary and that there was no harm in just one more e-mail exchange. Maybe he was just more cautious than the average guy, having been divorced, and that's why he needed a little more time to ask her out. Besides, he was so cute, there was no way she was letting this guy get away! "Maybe he will ask me out in the next e-mail and everything will work out just fine. Sometimes *The Rules* are just too strict," she told herself. But she told no one else, least of all us or her *Rules*-minded friends.

This time she waited 48 hours to respond, just to be more *Rules*-y: "I'm divorced about a year. New to online dating. Have met a few men. It's been fun."

Sadly, his fifth e-mail was "Do you know what you are looking for?"

Joanne decided to take matters into her own hands, thinking maybe he was shy or new to the Internet, so she decided to write back, "I'll know it when I see it. Maybe we can get together sometime. Here's my cell number."

He called the very next day.

See! Joanne told herself, *The Rules* are not written in stone, fourth e-mail, fifth e-mail, he answered her ad. All she did was give him her cell number without his having asked for it, what difference did that make? She cheated a little and it worked, that's all that mattered! She was walking on air.

The day he called, they spoke for a few minutes, but then he picked up his call waiting and abruptly got off the phone because he said his brother was on the other line long distance. He said he would call again. A few days later he left an upbeat message on her voice mail saying that he was looking forward to meeting her but that he was going on a business trip for a few days and would call when he got back. A week went by and another week and Joanne didn't hear from him. She checked her e-mail. Nothing! So she decided to e-mail him: "Hi, got your call. Hope your business trip went well."

Two days later he e-mailed her that his father was sick with pneumonia and that taking care of him was taking up all of his time. She e-mailed him back, "Sorry about your dad," and never heard from him again. No response. Poof! Gone!

Joanne called us, heartbroken. "How could this happen?" she wanted to know. "He seemed so interested in the beginning!"

We told her that we weren't thrilled with any of it. First of all, his questions were too deep and penetrating, not the kind a stranger should ask a woman in introductory e-mails and certainly not the kind a man asks when he wants to take you out, but more like the kind a pen pal or a therapist asks. And second, he never asked for her number; she volunteered it, trying to make things happen and that never works. We told her that whenever women don't play by *The Rules*, the men invariably are inundated with business trips, sick relatives, and all kinds of excuses!

We explained that the fourth e-mail rule was not arbitrary,

but based on many consultations. For some reason, we have found that if a man needs more than four e-mails to ask you out, he either has a girlfriend, is married, is a player, or is just not that interested. When a man is interested in dating, he will ask you out quickly, sometimes in the first e-mail. Four is the absolute cutoff. We told Joanne that had she followed *The Rules* to the letter, she would never have even spoken to him, gotten her hopes up, and wasted any time with this man. Maybe he was a player, maybe he was married. Who knows? *Rules* girls don't analyze why or how come, they just say, "Next!"

Like Joanne, other women have found heartache or were simply surprised at the results they got by breaking or even bending *The Rules* a little bit. Nancy's situation was different, but no better. The guy who answered her ad—a man she thought was insanely handsome—asked her out for Saturday night in his third e-mail. So far, so good.

But he sent the e-mail on Friday afternoon. She knew that the ask-by-Wednesday-for-a-Saturday-night-date *Rule* still applied to online dating as in real life, but she didn't care. She didn't want to say "Would love to, but I have plans" and not see him. She was feeling lonely since a recent breakup and wanted a Saturday night date no matter what. So she e-mailed him three hours later (as we've stated, bending one *Rule* leads to bending another!), "Saturday night sounds great!" He e-mailed back, "Okay, what is your number? I'll call you later and we can make plans."

That same night, he called her on her cell and they settled on a restaurant in her neighborhood. On Saturday afternoon he called to cancel, saying something had come up. She never heard from him again. We believe it is because it wasn't *The Rules* to begin with.

Debbie, 36, also bent a *Rule* and got hurt. A really nice-looking man answered her ad with, "You are a beautiful woman. I'm a doctor, 40, in pediatrics, I see kids every day and would love to have one of my own! Can we chat online sometime? What's a good time?" It was the best response she got out of 75 e-mails and she was thrilled! Trying to do *The Rules* after consulting with us, Debbie's answer was a vague, "Thanks. You are very sweet. Gee, I'm not sure. Every day is different."

That night she went online and forgot that we had told her to block herself. The nice-looking doctor Instant Messaged her immediately. She knew not to accept Instant Messages because they were too spontaneous and casual and not thought out, so she decided to ignore his Instant Message and log off, hoping that he would e-mail her instead. She checked her mail constantly for the next two days. Nothing. Thinking he may have felt she was rude not to Instant Message him back, she e-mailed him, "Sorry I couldn't chat the other night. Crazy deadlines at work."

The nice-looking doctor seemed happy to hear from her. He e-mailed her back five minutes later with, "Oh, I was wondering what happened. Maybe I can catch you online tonight?"

Debbie said, "Sure." (Bending one *Rule* leads to bending another!) She figured she would let him Instant Message her just this once to get the ball rolling and then block herself from that point on so he would be forced to e-mail her and maybe ask for her number.

That night he Instant Messaged her the second she got online.

DreamyDR40: *Hi gorgeous!*
PetiteBlonde36: *Hi!*

DreamyDR40: *So what's up?*

PetiteBlonde36: *Nothing much, long day at work.*

DreamyDR40: *So what kind of writer are you?*

PetiteBlonde36: *Travel writer, freelance.*

DreamyDR40: *Magazine, newspaper?*

PetiteBlonde36: *An in-flight travel magazine.*

DreamyDR40: *Do you travel a lot?*

PetiteBlonde36: *About once a month to the West Coast. What about you?*

DreamyDR40: *They don't let me out of the hospital. I haven't taken a vacation in three years. I'm kind of a workaholic.*

PetiteBlonde36: *Is that why you're online? No time for bar-hopping?*

DreamyDR40: *Exactly! So what's your story? Single, divorced?*

PetiteBlonde36: *Divorced two years, no kids.*

DreamyDR40: *Sorry, what happened?*

PetiteBlonde36: *Grew apart.*

DreamyDR40: *So where do you live? I forgot what you said in your ad.*

PetiteBlonde36: *Washington, D.C. What about you?*

DreamyDR40: *Boston. Does your magazine fly you out around here? Maybe you could visit me sometime.*

PetiteBlonde36: *No, just the West Coast, sorry.*

DreamyDR40: *Well, it's getting late, I'll let you go.*

Debbie was so taken aback by his ending their chat so soon that she didn't know what to say. She wanted to talk to him all night or at least until he asked for her number!

DreamyDR40: *Are you there, hon? Sweet dreams!*

PetiteBlonde36: *Good night!*

Debbie was bewildered, she didn't know what to think. She certainly didn't think she did anything wrong. So she told herself he must have had a long day at the hospital and just wanted to go to sleep. She was sure that he would e-mail her or Instant Message her the next day or very soon. She unblocked herself for the next five nights, but no Instant Messages and no e-mails. DreamyDR40 had poofed!

When Debbie contacted us, we told her that she should never have e-mailed him after his initial Instant Message, that if he was truly interested in her he would have Instant Messaged her again or e-mailed her to say, "Did you get my Instant Message?" and eventually ask her out. When he didn't even bother to contact her again after his initial Instant Message, he just wasn't that interested. Then when she e-mailed him, there was no challenge for him at all. And then the second he realized she wasn't going to fly to him, he ended their chat.

"But what about his first e-mail saying how beautiful I am? Doesn't that mean anything?" she asked.

Dime a dozen, we told her. The "Hello, gorgeous" or "Hi, beautiful" line is the biggest online cliché. Men say that all the time to get women hooked, and women end up getting hurt when they break *The Rules* with these online Don Juans.

The point of this chapter is to remind you that stricter is always better and that when you bend *The Rules* (in real life or online), the results follow suit. So if you want to break or even bend *The Rules* a little bit, realize that you are doing so at your own risk. If you want to be original, we suggest you be original at work or bake a cake that no one has baked before. But do not try to be original or unique with *The Rules*. Follow them to the letter if you want the best possible results!

Rules for Special Circumstances

The Rules for Long-Distance Online Relationships

"Be wary of the long-distance guy," says one veteran online *Rules* girl. "You never know if he has a wife back home or not, or if he is just into women visiting him (how convenient!) but would never travel to meet them. Remember, he's a complete stranger who happens to be literate."

Nevertheless, we hear about women falling in love with online guys all over the country and even the world, all the time. If you are one of them, what are the do's and don'ts?

The biggest mistake women are making in long-distance relationships is that they are hopping on planes to meet these online guys. Every woman who does this has a good reason, including:

- she just wants to get out of town
- she's a sight-seer, she wants to see that city
- she has frequent-flier miles

- she works for an airline
- she has friends, relatives, or business in that town
- her online guy is calling and e-mailing her a lot, so she figures he must be serious, so it's OK to fly to him first

Whatever the reason is, it is not *The Rules* if you agree to visit a man first under any circumstances, even if he pays for your travel expenses because, after all, that's only money, not time or energy spent. That puts you in the position of pursuer and allows him to be complacent. If he suggests you visit him and says he will show you around the town, politely decline with "Sounds great, but can't possibly get away" and cite work or personal reasons.

Do not suggest he visit you. He must think of that all by himself. If he doesn't suggest visiting you in his next e-mail, delete/next! He is not that interested. Visions of you are not keeping him up at night; he can take you or leave you and that is not what you want.

Indeed, long-distance courtships with good-looking strangers can be very enticing and equally heartbreaking, as Samantha, a graphic artist (ArtistGirl29) from San Francisco, found out. She met Peter, a bookstore owner (Bookish35) from London, in a chat room. He Instant Messaged her, "Hi, I'm Peter? What's your name? What kind of artist are you?" After chatting for about an hour about their backgrounds and love of the arts, Peter asked Samantha for her phone number and suggested exchanging photos. After that, he e-mailed her almost daily and called her about 20 times in two months. Peter thought Samantha was very pretty and asked her if she wanted to visit him in London. "I could show you all the great museums and art galleries," he said, "You could stay at my sister's flat if you are uncomfortable staying with me." Samantha had never been outside of the United States, so the prospect of touring London with this handsome Englishman sounded like something out of a romance novel.

She was about to say yes and buy roundtrip airline tickets, but she decided to check with her *Rules*-y girlfriend first, the one who had told her about online dating in the first place. "It's totally *The Rules*, he spoke to me first, he does all the calling, I've never called him once, I'm dying to see London, so can I go?" she said. Her friend hated to dampen Samantha's enthusiasm, but she told her the truth: "No, you can't go. He has to visit you three times before you visit him. That's the long-distance *Rule*. Otherwise the whole thing is too easy for him. Calling you a lot doesn't take a lot of effort and, for all you know, it may not cost him much, maybe he gets a cheap rate. He has to fly out to see you for you to know how serious he is. So just tell him something came up with work and you can't get away. See if he suggests visiting you, but don't tell him to. If he doesn't, then it's nothing!" ("Nothing" is what a *Rules* girl calls a non-relationship that is, in reality, nothing but fantasy on a woman's part.)

Samantha knew her girlfriend was right, and when Peter called later that night to discuss travel dates, she told him she couldn't make the trip. He was disappointed but did not suggest visiting her. He said, "Well, let me know when you can come to London." With that, he hung up and never called or e-mailed her again. Poof!

Had Samantha not consulted her friend and flown to London to visit Peter, she would have set a precedent for a lopsided long-distance relationship where he calls and e-mails a lot, but she is the one to pack a suitcase and hop on a plane.

Though she could rationalize traveling to see him anyway she likes—London is filled with culture and history; she has never been outside of the United States before; she has vacation days while Peter doesn't; he is willing to pay half her airfare; or she got a real bargain on a flight, etc.—the damage will have been done. Peter would know how much she liked him and could probably convince her to visit him again by saying "Next time we'll take the train to Bristol or Paris."

Usually when a woman visits a man first or once, it is like taking one sip or one bite of something delicious: It's never a one-time thing. She usually ends up visiting him three or four times until she realizes that he is using her and the relationship is not reciprocal. And it would have been just a fling for him and an exciting overseas boyfriend/serious relationship for her. So even a *Rules* beginning is no guarantee of anything if you defy the long-distance *Rules* and travel to him first.

For any online guy who, unlike Peter, does suggest visiting you, we say great, but proceed with caution, as you would for any date zero. Do not tell him where you live right away. Suggest a public place in which to meet, such as a restaurant or bar, that is convenient for you. If he flies in, do not pick him up at the airport; let him take a taxi, you are not a chauffeur or his girlfriend (yet). If he stays overnight, let him stay at a hotel. Even if he is coming cross-country, keep the first date to no more than five hours. Do not let it turn into a whirlwind weekend; do not feel obligated to show him around town or feel compelled to entertain him. You are not a tour guide. Do not take off from work to meet him, or he will know how much you like him. Just meet for lunch or dinner. Less is more.

If things go well and he visits you again, you can see him for a day. On his third visit, you can spend two days with him.

After three visits, you can visit him but only if he suggests it and hopefully he does. By this time, you're probably getting involved and you need to see him in his home environment to make sure he is who he says he is. So it's absolutely fine because you need to check him out, but don't make visiting him a habit. It is always a better visit when he has to pack a suitcase, fly or drive, and do all the work to see you.

The Rules screen out all the men who are just playing around and not serious about you.

Rules for Special Circumstances

The Rules for Older Online Daters

Online dating has proven to be a wonderful medium for all women, and especially women over 30, many of whom are divorced and not finding it easy to meet men anymore through conventional channels like blind dates and parties. When you're 23, you can go to a club or walk over to the twenty-something-year-old woman in the next cubicle and say, "Let's go for drinks after work." But when you're 35, 40, or 50, the man or woman in the cubicle next to yours is usually not available for drinks after work. He or she is probably 45 years old, and at 6 P.M., probably rushing home to be with his or her spouse or family in the suburbs.

So 30-plus-year-old women by the thousands are flocking to online dating services, which we think is smart as it exposes them to lots of men they would normally never meet. Why be alone just because you're too busy or tired to go to parties or clubs? The only problem is that some of the people using online dating are people who have been out of the dating loop for a decade or two. Divorced or never-married women may fall into the trap of using online dating to deal with loneliness, vent anger, air dirty laundry, and cry about their ex-boyfriend/ex-husband/financial woes, and other misfortunes because they think this is a way to find sympathy, resolve issues, or bond with men. This is a big mistake!

Online dating is not therapy! You should see a therapist, find a support group, or confide in good friends. Do not cast an online guy whom you hope to date into the role of savior, even if he initially encourages it or doesn't seem to mind your tales of woe. A man may be attentive, helpful, and compassionate in the beginning, but trust us, he will stop asking you out if you continue to whine, so don't go there!

Monica, 46, recently broke up with her boyfriend Don after a five-year going-nowhere relationship. Monica was so devastated by Don's infidelity—he was cheating on her with the 28-year-old cashier at his liquor store—that she refused to date or even meet men for a year because she no longer trusted them.

Monica's good friend, a single 39-year-old who was meeting lots of guys online, suggested Monica post an ad with her photo. "What have you got to lose? You've been alone for a year. You can't hide out for the rest of your life," she told her. When Monica hesitated, her friend said, "Just give me your best photo, I'll write the ad and post it for you. All you have to do is answer your mail."

Monica was pleasantly surprised to find 50 responses to her ad, SuddenlySingle46, a name she thought would let everyone know her plight and which would also help fuel further discussion on dates. One of them, Mark (OneForYou48), was just her type. She e-mailed him back and they started to correspond almost every day.

Monica thought Mark was a dream come true—he seemed really interested in her and asked a lot of questions. She was immediately honest with him about her ex-boyfriend's back-stabbing ways. Here is what she wrote:

SuddenlySingle46: *Not only did he leave me for a girl half his age, he showered her with gifts he couldn't afford—a fur coat, a diamond necklace—by going through money I loaned him to help him open his liquor store . . . $30,000. . . . Do you believe I have no proof as he doesn't like records, said that when it comes to business ventures I was more protected if there were no paper trails? I have no money and am working two jobs to pay the mortgage on a house we bought together. This is after being together five years!*

OneForYou48: *That's terrible. What a jerk. Good riddance. Have you been dating at all?*

SuddenlySingle46: *No, I just holed up at home for a year, crying myself to sleep. I just couldn't trust men anymore. I built a big wall around me that I'm trying to chip away at now, it's hard. A friend of mine suggested I do this, so here I am.*

OneForYou48: *Well, a pretty girl like you shouldn't be alone. Why don't we meet for drinks?*

SuddenlySingle46: *Sure.*

Monica and Mark met later that week. It was her first date in six years. She continued the tell-all and went on and on about how her biggest regret in life was not having children, that her ex-boyfriend didn't want kids and now she knows it's because he was never planning to marry her. She also told Mark that she decided to cancel her cable TV subscription and let her gym membership go because she couldn't afford either, but that she was hoping to get a raise at the law firm where she worked as a paralegal so she could pay off some credit card debt. "I haven't bought anything in a year—not one piece of clothing, not a lipstick, nothing, that's how bad things have been," she told him.

Mark, a financial analyst, listened politely. He thought Monica was very pretty, but her sob stories were becoming a real downer. He had thought about suggesting dinner, but changed his mind and ended the date first.

Monica e-mailed him the next day, "Thanks for drinks, it was nice meeting you, you are very sweet and a great listener (not like my ex). Have a great day."

Mark didn't e-mail back for a week, so Monica e-mailed him again, "Is everything OK? Would love to hear from you."

The next day, Mark decided to e-mail her back a white lie: "You seem like a nice person, but I recently met someone and I don't want to date anyone else right now. Good luck!"

Monica was so hurt she called her friend and said, "See, this is exactly why I don't want to meet men. I thought he was going to be different, special, but he turned out to be just like every other guy. . . ."

"But he thought you were beautiful, what happened? You didn't tell him about your breakup, did you?" her friend asked.

"Of course I did, what else was I going to talk about? He asked me many questions. He wanted to know about it," Monica replied.

"Did you talk about it a little or a lot?" her friend asked.

"A lot, just about every e-mail, Instant Message, on our

drink date I told him about my finances. Did you really expect me to talk about current events when my life is falling apart?" said Monica, brushing away a tear.

Of course, the answer to Monica's question is, unfortunately, yes. We know breaking up a long-term relationship can be emotionally and sometimes financially painful, but we also know that talking about it during the crucial first two months of dates and e-mails with a man is premature. Cry before you log on, cry after you log off, cry on the way to a drink date, cry on the way home, but *do not go on and on about your horrible ex online or during the date.* No matter how bad things are, you still have to be a CUAO, a princess on dates, not someone looking for a savior. Even if, as you are typing, the heat is turned off because you didn't pay your gas bill, and the creditors are knocking on your door, you still e-mail back, "Let's see, I love to ski, play tennis, and see Meg Ryan movies." This will be an acting job for sure, especially if you have been burnt badly, but if you wear your heart on your sleeve, you will definitely be all alone. Remember, nobody wants you when you're down and out!

Katie, 37, was in a similar situation as Monica, only worse: She had three kids ages eight to thirteen, and her husband left her for a less attractive, older, wealthy woman he had met on a business trip. Katie was heartbroken and also frantic about how she would make ends meet and take care of her children. On top of that, she was worried about how dating would affect her kids since they adored their father. These were the thoughts that whirled in Katie's head everywhere she went. She told perfect strangers on supermarket lines and at PTA meetings, anyone who would listen, about her pain and her fears.

Six months after her divorce became final, these thoughts

still plagued her, but at a neighbor's suggestion, she decided to post an ad and photo on an online dating service. She called herself BeautifulLady37. She got about 70 responses in the first month. Once she got into e-mail or Instant Message exchanges with men, they would invariably ask, "So what happened with your marriage?"

She basically told them everything: How her husband had illegally broken into their IRAs and used the money to trade in the stock market; that when the market crashed, he left her for an older, richer woman; that he was a good father but a lousy husband, and so on. Katie would also mention that he recently reduced her settlement and when she complained, he screamed, "Why don't you get a better paying job?" She told her dates, "I can't believe how mean he is!"

One by one, the online guys seemed sympathetic, then poofed! Katie didn't understand why until she contacted us and we told her, "You can't talk about your divorce. You're scaring these guys away. Be light and breezy. Tell them when you've known them five or six months."

Desperate to date again, Katie listened. When she felt like saying in an e-mail to a guy who asked about her divorce, "My ex is a dirtbag. He switched the car payments into my name while we were still married," she said, "We just grew apart."

When she felt like saying that she didn't know how she was going to pay the mortgage and that her kids missed their father, she said, "Things have been hectic lately, sorry I couldn't get back to you sooner." (Things were not really hectic; on the contrary, many days it was all she could do to make the kids' lunches without crying.) Even when the online guys were e-mailing her about their exes, she did not reciprocate, keeping her e-mails light and breezy.

To be sure, Katie cried before and after she logged on, but forced herself to be a CUAO online. After a couple of months, she received an e-mail from Mike, HandsomePilot42, to whom she was immediately attracted.

After three e-mail exchanges, he asked for her number, called the next day, and asked her out for Friday night. Katie wore a short skirt and high heels, and even though she wanted to cry as she was getting dressed, she forced herself not to, lest it ruin her mascara. She didn't say anything about her divorce or her finances for three hours, even though that was all she could think about. Rather than poof!, Mike asked her out at the end of the date. Katie had to admit this light and breezy stuff worked.

Afraid to make any mistakes, Katie read the chapter in our first book about *Rules* for divorced women with kids. Therefore, she knew she should always put her kids first and Mike second, no matter how lonely she felt. Sometimes as badly as she wanted to talk to Mike when he called, if her kids were home, she forced herself to say, "Would love to talk, but my kids are here . . . so it's really not a good time."

She was also careful not to say anything about sex on the phone with him when her kids were around because they could be on a phone extension. She also refrained from writing anything steamy or revealing in her e-mails just in case her kids figured out her password and read them, or even looked at her screen during the five minutes it took her to go to the bathroom.

Katie was also polite in that she didn't call Mike when he was with his kids. She had heard of women forcing men to "merge families" and knew from *The Rules* that this was not the way to go. She was wise enough to know that you could feel like two teenagers in love, but if you are a parent, you are the only role model that your children have, so she made sure not to act like a teen!

Now, Katie's been dating Mike for months, he e-mails her every other day or so and tries not to call her when her children are home. The best part is that Katie rarely thinks about her ex anymore. It's true, living well and falling in love with someone else is the best revenge!

Rules for Special Circumstances

10 Tips for Teenage Daters

You're a teenager, so perhaps your older sister or mother bought you this book or you came across it in the bookstore. You're flipping through it, thinking, "This is not for me. I'm only 16. I'm not allowed to talk to strangers, only people I know from school or camp. I'm not allowed to go into chat rooms. I don't have an ad online. I don't want to get married. Give me a break. I'll read it when I'm 23."

But then you flip through the book once more and you have to admit that you have been e-mailing this cute guy in your class hoping he will ask you to the movies—you even sent him a photo of you in a bikini with your camp friends—and that you stayed online with him for two hours the other night in an Instant Message chat that you initiated, and so you didn't finish your homework, and, truth be told, you're kind of addicted to the computer. Every day you come home, throw your coat on the floor, and log on. You're so busy on the computer that you don't even hear your mother scream, "Dinner is ready. Finish your homework. Clean your room."

No, you're not posting ads or looking for a husband, but you are looking to date or have a boyfriend, or you just want to be popular, and we're here to tell you that you will never get it by e-mailing boys first or chatting with them all night. *The Rules* are not just about getting married, but about avoiding guy pain. Left to your own devices, you are destined for heartache. Guys don't date the girls that Instant Message them and chat all night; they want the ones who are busy and log off first.

Besides, if you break *Rules* at 16, you might continue to do so at 23 and 35 when you may very well want to date with self-esteem, to be popular, to be sought after by men, maybe to get married. Why not form good dating habits now so that you carry them over into your twenties and thirties?

Here are 10 teen tips:

1. Start to be a teen Creature Unlike Any Other, (CUAO) now. Being a CUAO is an attitude, a state of mind. You don't have to be the prom queen or the smartest in your class to feel good about yourself. Tell yourself that you are beautiful inside and out and that any boy would be lucky to sit next to you in class, eat lunch with you, or take you ice skating or to the movies. Of course, it helps to do the right thing. Teen CUAOs are happy campers; they eat right, exercise, do their homework, listen to their parents, and they don't smoke cigarettes, do drugs, or have sex. They also believe that boys should pursue them, not vice versa.

2. Only e-mail or Instant Message other teens *you* already know from school, camp, and after-school activities—not friends of friends and absolutely no strangers.

3. Don't e-mail or Instant Message your crush first or volunteer your phone number. He has to ask for it.

4. Don't have your best friends Instant Message or e-mail your crush's best friends to ask if he likes you. Let his friends be the ones to do all the asking of *your* friends.

5. If you can't be online without Instant Messaging your crush first, then take him off your Buddy List! Ask your friends not to tell you when he's online, so you won't be tempted. Ignorance is bliss.

6. Try not to chat with your crush in an Instant Message he initiated for more than 30 minutes (and at most, an hour), and make sure you end the Instant Message first.

7. Don't neglect your homework or other responsibilities to chat online.

8. Hit delete or cancel and don't respond when a guy talks about sex.

9. Don't copy and paste and forward e-mails between you and your crush to your three best friends. One will surely forward it to her best friends and it could be forwarded to your whole class or even the whole school. In the same vein, don't write anything in an Instant Message or e-mail that you wouldn't want to be broadcast on speaker-phone to your whole school, such as who you secretly like or don't like, or who you think is cute or not cute. Teenagers are not the best keepers of secrets. Everything you write can be saved and printed out, so you won't be able to deny it. Who needs to be embarrassed?

10. Never give your boyfriend or a friend your pass-word, because if you fight or break up and forget to change

it, it could be a bad scene. Same goes for a friend; you don't know what they will do with it!

This is the kind of advice we give to teenagers who write to us. For example, we recently received a letter from Brandy, a 16-year-old from Wichita, who saw *The Rules* mentioned on a TV show. Here is what she wrote:

Dear Ellen and Sherrie,

My name is Brandy. I am 16 and in 10th grade. I saw The Rules *mentioned on 7th Heaven and ran out and bought your book. I thought maybe you could help me.*

I've had this serious crush on this guy Chad in my class for about a year. He is really cute with curly blond hair. He's really athletic. A couple of weeks ago he came up to me after class and asked me if I would help him with a project. I said sure. He asked me for my e-mail address and said he would send me what he had written so far. The next day he e-mailed me and I e-mailed him back with some suggestions. He e-mailed back "Thanks." I haven't heard from him since.

Since he spoke to me first, would it be okay to e-mail him, "How did the project go?" I put him on my Buddy List and see him a lot online. Can I Instant Message him something like, "Want to go to the movies" or tell him that I like him? How can I get him to ask me out? Help!

Brandy

We wrote Brandy back the following:

Dear Brandy,

Sorry, you can't! Don't e-mail him again. Yes, he spoke to you first, but about schoolwork, not dating you. He is not romanti-

cally interested in you. Next! Unfortunately, dating only works when a boy asks a girl out. If he wanted to see a movie with you, he would have asked you already. So you are just going to have to wait for some other guy who does ask you out.

P.S. Never tell a guy online that you like him or anything else that you don't want the whole school to know. He could forward it to his friends and they could forward it to their friends and before you know it, your whole grade will know your little secret. Be discreet! Good luck!

Ellen and Sherrie

Rules for Special Circumstances

Online Dating for Recognizable Personalities

Yes, even recognizable personalities are using online dating. They, like the rest of us, sometimes have a hard time meeting the opposite sex through regular channels and have found online dating a viable alternative.

We interviewed three recognizable women who put their ads up on various services. Only one of them, the most famous of the three, chose not to post her photo. All three would have good reason not to do online dating at all because they are well known. But, being pragmatic and wanting to change their single status, they decided to put aside their egos and try it, only to discover that they actually liked it and, more important, met quality men!

One celebrity, a very attractive comedienne, decided to try online dating after her marriage of 18 years ended. Although this is only one avenue she is using to meet men, she is a big enthusiast. She told us:

The wells of introduction had dried up. I had wonderful experiences in the sixties and seventies with blind dates. I don't see a huge difference between this and blind dates. I met my husband when he sent me a fan letter with a picture. I contacted him at his office, made a dinner date, got married, and had a baby. What's the difference between fan mail and online dating? When you meet someone it's usually blind anyway, you've never met them before, unless you meet at a party. Besides, I have an adventurous spirit at this juncture in my life and I was not going to go gently into the night. I am not taking a good book to bed like some friends of mine who would never do online dating.

To women who worry that online dating is unsafe, she laughs. She found the opposite to be true—that men want to correspond endlessly and take forever to ask for her number, much less arrange to meet her. "These guys are far from predators. Many are actually afraid to meet. They want to connect but they are scared of their own shadows. I had one guy who lives in New York City ask me, where is Tavern on the Green [a well-known Manhattan restaurant]? Come on . . . I dropped him immediately."

To friends of hers who shy away from the Internet, she simply tells them, "Just check it out. You can have a terrifying experience with someone you *do* know." On the other hand, she takes every precaution. Her phone number is unlisted, she gives out only her cell phone number, and she did not post a photo with her ad even though she knew it would mean fewer responses. She advises other celebrities to do the same.

True, I'm not as famous as Julia Roberts or Meg Ryan, but if the men don't know who I am, I love it. I don't want them to contact me just for my celebrity. I love the game. When they know who I am, then I become a trophy. They become overwhelmed. I need a man who can handle my fame.

Typically, a man will recognize who she is on their first date and gush, "Wow, I can't believe it's you, why would you go out with me?"

Her answer: "Don't ask why. It's rare to find someone who shares the love of the arts."

She doesn't want a man overwhelmed by her achievements, just a man. "I'm a woman, I'm a mom, I get cramps and headaches," she explains.

Her ad simply says she is a "known quantity" and that is why she is not including her photo. She describes herself as an artist/painter/musician which intrigues a lot of men. Many of the responses she's received were from men who wanted to figure out who she is and much of the correspondence became a guessing game. She also included a quiz in her profile because she only wanted to meet men who shared her love of the arts. Some of the questions: Name two jazz artists. Name three directors. Who is Vermeer?

About eight out of 10 respondents guessed her identity. After about four e-mail exchanges, she would give them her cell number and agree to meet at a public place such as Le Cirque in Manhattan.

Some sent her photos, some did not. "I'm not fair. They can speak to me on the phone or see me on the date. I don't believe in sending my picture. But I want to know what they look like. I'd be lying if I said physical appearance isn't important. Some looked like the Cookie Monster. I'm looking for an attractive, clean-cut man . . . and I read their profiles carefully to make sure we have something in common like music and the arts."

She agreed to meet a man to whom she was not that attracted, who then became a friend. "I believe we meet people for a reason, both friends and potential lovers."

While she has yet to meet a man she is exclusive with on the Internet, she has had several flirtations and some romantic liaisons. "I don't harbor this 'soul mate' crap. I don't believe that is the point of it all, rather to get back into the swing of things, to connect, to have fun."

Another well-known person was willing to share her experience. Julie (not her real name) has a radio show three times a week in which she talks about personal finance. She isn't easily recognizable, but she is well known in her field. She posted an ad with her photo and the response was good. She had no qualms about online dating. After all, she was in her forties with two kids. As she explained,

Where am I supposed to go to meet new men? I'm in the same predicament as everyone else; the minute my radio show is over, I get into my car and shoot home so I can be there for my two middle-school-aged children. The bars have nothing but alcoholics; they aren't there to meet women, they just want to sit on a bar stool and drink!

Now I am having so many dates and so much fun. My non-Internet divorced friends in the same situation haven't had a real date in a year in some cases, but me, I am meeting a lot of interesting men all the time. I even have a great trick to get extra dates. Sometimes when I have to fly to New York or Chicago to do publicity or to interview someone, I post my ad in those areas for a week or two and invariably get responses from men who want to meet for dinner or drinks while I'm in town. The last time I went to DC to visit my married sister, her husband and kids, my sister and her family couldn't believe I had a drink date Friday night. I posted my ad there a week or two before I was going to be in town. I'm still doing *The Rules* as they are still seeking me out, but it enables me to meet all sorts of people.

For me, it has been absolutely life-changing. I am a bit shy—I know, I know, I'm on the radio, but that's show business. In real life, I am very private and no one recognizes me, and, until I know these guys better, I say I am in finance. My advice is: post your photo. Who cares who you are? Get over it, girls, and have fun!

One doesn't have to be famous to be concerned about one's public position. For example, we also asked Elizabeth, a PTA mom, 38, with three little kids in school, who was recently separated after 10 years of marriage and who is well known in her community—she was class mother—why she was doing online dating. Did she feel embarrassed? She admitted that at first she felt some apprehension, especially about the photo part, but after a few not-so-great responses to an ad without a photo, she figured it was time to let loose and post her picture. Elizabeth is 5'2", perky with blue eyes, and she knew in her heart that part of what had drawn men to her in the past was her good looks. She decided she couldn't worry about what everyone thought, she had to do what she had to do.

After posting her photo, a cute single dad with kids in the same school responded. His first e-mail to her was, "Hey, I didn't know you were single . . . this is a great day!" He asked her out for dinner. She met him at the restaurant and felt immediately comfortable, as they remembered each other from the end-of-the-year school picnic. They just hadn't realized they were both unattached. Their first date was great, but as she was recently separated, she kept her ad up and forced herself to go out with other men who responded to her ad, including a doctor, a plumber, and a CPA, all divorced men with kids in her area. She eventually settled on the first guy as she liked him the best and he asked her to be exclusive. Best of all, not one person in the PTA or anyone else she knew ever mentioned her ad or anything about online dating.

All of these recognizable women were humble enough (and adventuresome enough) to try online dating, so their advice to women in their position is, "Put aside your pride and try it!"

Most Frequently Asked Questions and Consultations

Q: With online dating, when do *The Rules* begin? With the first date or first e-mail?

A: The first e-mail. Do not wait until you have a date with him to do *The Rules*. If a man responds to your ad and photo, *The Rules* begin the second he notices your ad and e-mails you. You must wait 24 hours to respond, keep your e-mails short, and do every other *Rule* we say in this book. In a chat room, *The Rules* begin with your chat room behavior as soon as you go in, even before his first Instant Message to you. For example, you don't enter a chat room and say, "Any available men in here?" In addition, when a man writes in a chat room something like, "Any available women in here?" you don't respond, saying, "Me!" You keep talking about the general topic, and let him Instant Message you specifically. After 10 or 15 minutes chatting back and forth, you need to say you have to get going. Hopefully, he will ask you out or ask for your telephone number at the end of the chat, or else you have to wait for him to e-mail you and ask you out.

Q: If I don't answer every e-mail, won't a man think I don't like him, especially if he sends me a joke?

A: No, he will just think you are busy, that you have a life, and that you aren't frantically checking your e-mails every minute. He'll probably wonder where you are, who you are going out with, if the other guy or guys are better looking or drive sportier cars, and what he has to do to get your attention (an even funnier joke or an e-mail bouquet) and when, if ever, you'll e-mail him back. Or he'll think about e-mailing you again or even calling you!

Q: My boyfriend and I met through an online dating service. When people ask how we met, should I tell them? I'm kind of embarrassed about it.

A: Five years ago we might have told you to say you met "through friends," but not anymore. There's nothing to be embarrassed about now. Millions of men and women are meeting this way every day. It is no more contrived than a blind date or a singles dance. Besides, if the person asking you is single, you will actually be doing him or her a favor by telling them that online dating is a viable way to meet. After all, you are a success story!

Q: When I talk to guys in chat rooms and they start to make inappropriate sexual innuendoes, what should I do? Is there a way for me to steer the conversation around?

A: Don't answer. If they are not smart enough to say when you don't answer back, "Have I offended you?" then they are not smart enough to ever talk to you again. Hit cancel and wait for another guy to Instant Message or e-mail you.

Q: How will my personality shine through if I can't write an in-depth description of what I want in a man in my ad and my e-mails have to be short and sweet?

A: Unfortunately, you cannot fit your whole personality into an ad or a photo or a few e-mails; your ad and e-mails are just the beginning, a mere glimpse of who you are. While the Internet allows you to meet men, it is not a shortcut to intimacy. A man still has to take you out on dates to learn more about you. Besides, women write all sorts of things like "I want a man 40–50 years old who is financially successful and likes swing dancing" and still get responses from men in their thirties who are unemployed and can't dance. You get what you get and then you pick and choose the ones you want. That's just the way it is.

Q: What if an online guy e-mails me, "Loved your ad, When is a good time to chat online?" What do I write back?

A: Don't tell him "I don't chat online" or "I don't accept Instant Messages," just say something like, "My schedule is crazy lately. Every day is different, just not sure." And then when he realizes that you won't make an appointment for an online chat, he will have to e-mail you and eventually ask for your telephone number to make a date. If he doesn't e-mail you, he was not that interested, just killing time.

Q: If a guy who answered your ad says he'd love to chat and gives you his number, is it okay to call him?

A: No, wait 24 hours and then e-mail him back, "Chatting sounds good, here's my number," and give him your cell number. He has to call you. There's no way to tell if a man is going to call you unless he calls you. It is very common for women to give men their cell numbers and they still don't call.

Q: I've had a couple of online guys suggest meeting at Starbucks for the first time. I thought that was kind of cheap. Can I say I'd rather not meet at a coffee place?

A: A coffee date for the first meeting is actually a good idea because it keeps the date to an hour or two, which is all you want it to be. Also, these places are usually crowded, well lit, and safe, perfect for meeting a stranger. It is not a sign that he is cheap, but practical. There is probably a Starbucks near you and that is where you want to meet. But if he wants to take you to Starbucks for your second date, then he is cheap!

Q: What if a guy asks you for drinks and then after you meet him he asks you to have dinner that night as well? Is that OK?

A: No. Say you would love to, but you have to get going. It's a good sign that he asked and an even better sign that you say no. You're not much of a challenge if he can see more of you at the last minute. If he wants to have dinner with you, he has to ask you out on another date.

Q: In his profile, he says he's "undecided" about kids. Can I bring this up on our first date? I'm 34 and definitely want to have a kid or two. I don't want to waste my time with a guy who doesn't!

A: Definitely not! Remember you didn't read his profile, you barely scanned it. *Rules* girls never bring up marriage, kids, future—the man has to. Just be light and breezy and eventually you will find out where he stands on kids when he brings it up. Get to know him a bit first; if you ask him a question about your or his biological clock on date zero, he is sure to poof!

Q: If I take 24 hours to answer men's e-mails, won't they move on to the other 20 women who are answering their e-mails right away?

A: No, the race doesn't go to the swiftest here. If a guy thinks you are pretty, he will wait a day to hear from you. He may even think you are busy with work or other men and that will be good for him in terms of the chase. Don't worry about what other women are doing. If they are answering men right away, they are probably doing other things right away, and it won't work long-term.

Q: I met a man online in a romance chat room. He Instant Messaged me first. I live in Denver. He lives in San Francisco. He's 39, and I'm 35 and in the process of ending my marriage. We've been e-mailing and calling each other for months, he says he loves me, but he's afraid to take the relationship to the next level (meeting each other) because he's afraid my feelings for him might change if we meet, that I might break his heart, and go back to my husband. Any suggestions?

A: Stop e-mailing him. He is a buyer beware. If a man doesn't want to meet you after months of e-mails, he is either married, involved, or looks or is nothing like his photo and ad and doesn't want you to find out. And FYI, any man who says I love you before you meet him cannot be taken seriously. His insecurities may be too great for him to overcome. If everybody refused to meet because of such fears, online relationships would never leave the computer. People have all sorts of fears, but they meet anyway. So our advice is No Contact, do not e-mail him or call him or return his e-mails and calls, so that he is forced to suggest meeting you, or not!

Q: If he talks about his ex, can I talk about my ex?

A: No, definitely not on the first six dates. The reason is, if your exes become the topic of conversation, you don't know whether he is using you as a therapist or trying to gather information on how women think or what. Besides, women have told us that when they start talking about their exes they can't stop; it's too seductive, like a drug, so it's for your own good not to. Four words you should never use in an ad or in real life with a man are "commitment," "soul mate," and "ex-boyfriend" or "ex-husband." And buyer beware, if he really likes you and feels a spark, he would not want to talk about his ex at all. He would want to know more about you.

Q: I've been in an e-mail relationship with a man I met in a writers' chat room three months ago. He Instant Messaged me first and we exchanged headshots. I found him to be extremely good-looking. Now we e-mail each other every day. So far he's content to be friends and has not asked to meet even though we live only a half hour apart. A friend of mine suggested I send him another photo of me when I worked as a swimsuit model to turn him on. Do you think that will help? Or do you think that will ruin our friendship?

A: It won't help, so do not send him the photo. If he was not interested in your first photo enough to ask you out, then he's not interested in you period. Besides, if you send him another (unsolicited) photo, he will know you like him and that you want more. And if the photo is sexy, he may get the wrong idea and meet you just for sex. Try to accept that he is not romantically interested in you. You can continue to be friends with him and enjoy it for what it is. At the same time, post an ad with your photo and wait for men to e-mail you who are interested in actually meeting you and having a real relationship, and not just a pen-pal relationship.

Q: A really cute guy answered my ad and wanted to meet me right away. I had already met someone else and said I was busy. Then two months later I broke up with that guy and e-mailed the really cute guy and told him about my breakup and asked if we could get together. He said great but now he wants me to call him and get directions so I can drive to him. He lives four hours away. What should I do?

A: It was a bad idea to e-mail him about your breakup and to suggest getting together. You gave too much information and took away the chase. OK, you're available now, but you could have just e-mailed him, "Hey, how have you been? I know you live up north, how's the weather there?" Then he could have e-mailed back, "Want to get together?" Now he knows you are eager and interested and that you will drive to him. So here's your plan: Do not call him. E-mail him that you will not be able to drive to him, you just can't get away, work, car trouble, whatever. In addition, do not suggest he drive to you. He has to suggest that. Maybe he is seeing someone now. Who knows? If he doesn't suggest coming to you, next!

Q: We met online in a chat room. He Instant Messaged me first and we exchanged photos. He said "wow" and suggested meeting. We have been dating for three months, but I don't see him every weekend because he travels for work sometimes or has his kids. He catches me in Instant Messages every day and that's also how he asks me out on dates. Is this OK?

A: Not great. Too easy and casual for him. Better to block yourself so he can't Instant Message you. Catching you online is too casual, like dropping by your house or your office and getting to be with you instantly without any effort, without having to wonder and wait. It's too easy. You need to be more of a challenge. If you block yourself, he will be forced to e-mail you and wait 24 hours to hear back from you or, better yet, ask you out at the end of dates. Try this experiment: Don't be online for a couple of weeks and see if he e-mails. Honestly, this guy does not sound like a potential husband. Date others since he is not asking you out every weekend anyway.

Q: I met a man online, he answered my ad and asked me out after three e-mails. We met for dinner and sparks flew and we ended up sleeping together. The next day he e-mailed me "Had a nice time last night, but why don't we take things slow." Of course, I wanted him to say "You are beautiful and last night was magnificent, when can I see you again?" I'm so hurt. Was this a one-night stand? What should I e-mail him back?

A: When you sleep with a man on the first date, you are basically kissing the relationship good-bye 99 percent of the time, so we wish you luck! When a man says he wants space, especially right after having sex with you, it is not a good sign. We say, next! But if you are determined to turn the tables on him, we suggest doing *The Rules* strictly from this moment on. Do not answer his e-mail at all or any other e-mails if they are just commentary. Let him ask you out twice more before you say OK. So even though you slept with him, at least he will think that you are not one of those women who think, "Now that we have slept together, this is a relationship." No, you are going to be just the opposite, the girl who has sex on the first date (just this once) but doesn't care about a relationship, just like a man, just like him! If this relationship continues, never e-mail him back unless it is about a date and turn him down here and there for dates and end the dates first.

Q: I saw his profile on a dating website two months ago and answered his ad. He asked to see my photo. He said he thought I was pretty. He writes me long adoring e-mails and we Instant Message and call each other all the time and talk about everything and anything like best friends. We've also had cybersex. I told him I am recently out of a relationship and then he said let's not rush things. I said, no, I am totally fine and why don't we meet soon? He said he values our friendship, too much is at stake, and he doesn't want to be the rebound guy. What should I do?

A: Unfortunately, you broke every *Rule* by answering his ad, chatting up a storm, and suggesting getting together. We know you think you have something more than special here, a soul-mate thing, a bond that can't be broken beyond time and space, but this man is only interested in an online friendship and cybersex—which is not *The Rules!* You must understand that when a man really likes you, he wants to see you, hold your hand, and be in the same room with you on Saturday nights. Don't be fooled by his kindness. A lot of men are brought up by their mothers to be polite, so that when a woman e-mails them, they say "Wow, you're beautiful" and then talk about valuing your friendship (yeah, right!). Do not believe his excuse that he doesn't want to ruin your friendship or be the rebound guy. Accept this relationship for what it is (pen pals) and, hopefully, don't put all your energy there if you want a real relationship. Stay friends or not, but keep your ad and photo up and wait for men to e-mail you who really do want to meet you!

Q: I answered his ad and we corresponded for about a month and were supposed to meet—we live three hours away from each other—when he pulled back and said he wasn't ready. I was devastated. After two weeks of No Contact, I e-mailed him and said why don't we meet first and see what happens. I drove halfway to him and then we decided to spend the week-end at his place—no sex—and he seemed totally smitten. He invited me to visit him again but said he first needs to break up with another woman. I know I have broken some *Rules*. Is it too late for him to think of me as unattainable?

A: Yes, it's over, he is not interested; he was happy to spend the weekend with you, but that's it, there's nothing here. Because you answered his ad and were the one to suggest meeting and then met him halfway and spent the weekend—that's four *Rules* broken right there!—this relationship will never be anything because he is not interested. He has already hurt you twice in the month you have known him. In the future, don't answer a man's ad. Instead, post an ad with your photo and let men e-mail you and ask you out. Do not meet them halfway. They must meet you at a public place near you.

We have no hope for this relationship, but you can try this and see what happens: Do not e-mail this guy again and answer once for every three of his e-mails, just the ones about dates, not chit-chat. He must suggest seeing you again, but you absolutely cannot visit him at his place or meet him halfway again. Say you are busy with work or can't leave your dog and can't possibly get away. If he doesn't come to you, the relationship is over. Next!

Q: I answered his ad and told him to check out my ad and if he was interested to e-mail me. He was interested and gave me his number to call him. We talked on the phone for two hours and decided to meet at a coffee shop. When I saw him, I thought, "no way" because he was older and not as good-looking as his photo. He definitely was taken by my looks and asked me out again. I thought, "What have I got to lose?" But on the second date, I thought he was kind of cute and slept with him. I know, bad idea! Anyway, now it's nine months later and we're seeing each other all the time and I'm obsessed with marrying him but he says I'm smothering him and he's asking for space. He is divorced two years with no kids. Can I still do *The Rules?*

A: Because you answered his ad and then called him first, thus initiating this relationship, it will most likely never be anything. Having sex on the second date, seeing him all the time, and then having him tell you he feels smothered is not something *Rules* girls do or hear. When a man says you are smothering him, it's time to leave town.

But if you don't believe us, you can find out for yourself. Start practicing *The Rules* now on him and see what happens. Leave him alone and see how he feels about you. Do not call or e-mail him and only return calls and e-mails about dates. Give him space, let him chase you. See him only once a week—Saturday night—if he asks by Wednesday. Turn him down for any other night of the week. At the same time, post an ad with your photo and wait for men to e-mail you and then do all the other *Rules* for online dating in this book.

Q: How can I increase the number of men who respond to my ad?

A: You can't. That's like saying how can I increase the number of men who speak to me first at a party. If you write a light and breezy ad and post your best headshot and still don't get a lot of responses, just tell yourself it's not your time. Non-*Rules* girls may put in busty headshots and flirtatious copy to entice more men, but this doesn't work long-term.

Q: If you're in a relationship and you've slept together and he's even said I love you but hasn't said you are exclusive, how do you know if you are exclusive or can date others?

A: You don't. Just date others (or not) until he says you are exclusive. Don't bring it up or drop hints to get him to discuss it. For example, don't say, "I have a date Friday night, is that OK?" You probably are exclusive, but it's always better when he asks you to be exclusive, not when you have to ask "Are we exclusive?"

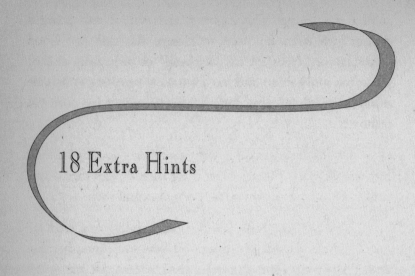

18 Extra Hints

1. Cast a wide net. If you live in a tiny town where the dating pool is small or you are not happy with the responses you are getting in your area, do not feel you have to post locally. You can post in a bigger city or nationally. Some dating services list you by your area code or ZIP code so you can put yourself in another area, such as where you grew up, or where you have friends or relatives, or where you might want to live someday. Don't worry. If a guy likes your photo and ad, enjoys e-mailing and calling you, he will fly out to meet you.

2. Find out if you can update your ad on your service so you come up as new, since some men will only browse through the most recent ads.

3. Don't change the subject title at the top of an e-mail that he sent to you, where it says SUBJ: (subject title), Date, From, and To. Just hit the reply button. Woman agonize too much over what to write to a man to begin with. For example, if the

subject says "Happy Thanksgiving" and you are responding a day or two later, no need to change the title to "Good Morning" or "Plans for the Weekend" or something else. It shows too much effort and interest to keep updating every title of every e-mail you send him. Let him notice it (or not) and change it.

4. No need to thank a guy the day after a date by sending him a smiley face :) (that's a colon and a close parenthesis) or a coffee cup greeting or anything! Let him e-mail you.

5. Do not sign "love" or even "luv" unless and until he does. There is a tendency to sign off with something because e-mail is in letter form, but don't until he does. He has to say "love" first, even online.

6. We are not big fans of Instant Message conversations, but if you find yourself in one, count to 20 before you push send. Pausing like that is good because it creates space between you and a man and makes him not so sure how interested you are, which makes him want to chat with you more. Besides, every other girl is responding in nanoseconds, so you'll stand out!

7. Another Instant Message trick is to not respond at all at some point in the conversation until he Instant Messages you again with another comment or perhaps a question like, "Are you still there?" If he thinks you are busy or preoccupied, all the better.

8. A man who doesn't show up or cancels date zero is always a delete/next!

9. Don't use special typeface, i.e., boldface, script, interesting color, etc. It screams that you are trying too hard!

10. If you are posting on a message board, stick to the topic and never respond to a man's posts, for example, don't say "I agree with Stuart22, who said Gore should have won." Just say, "Gore should have won." Let Stuart22 e-mail you, "Wow, we think alike!"

11. Form a buddy system with a friend or relative who you can talk to or e-mail about your online dating adventures, or call or e-mail a *Rules* contact. You do not have to do online dating alone. Remember, two minds are better than one and you are often your own worst enemy.

12. Don't believe everything you read about online dating. A recent magazine article suggested that women e-mail men back "right away" because busy men like a quick response. Here's what we think about that: Men also like to have sex on the first date, but *Rules* girls don't do that either.

13. If you are asked in a questionnaire what you prefer a man's marital status to be, do not check off single, divorced, separated, and widower. It looks overanxious. Just select single or divorced or whatever status you are and you will get single, separated, and widowers anyway.

14. When a man calls for the first time after a few e-mails, do not stay on the phone for more than 10 minutes; 20 minutes is the absolute limit. The first call is just to hear his voice, so that you know he is real, not to discuss his last three relationships or yours, or his feelings about marriage. The first call is just to secure a date, time, and place for meeting, that's it. Remember, you can talk for an hour or two on the date. So after 10 to 20 minutes, just say there's my doorbell or I was just on my way out. It's not *Rules*-y to spend two hours on the

phone, especially with someone you have not even met yet. Even though you have not gone to date zero with someone, *The Rules* have begun!

15. If you have a girlfriend who is also doing online dating, join the same service so you can see if the same men e-mail both of you and say the same thing. If they do, then you can put it in the back of your head that they may not be that serious. Chances are they probably e-mailed 20 other women the same thing!

16. If you are in an established relationship and you have a choice of calling or e-mailing him, e-mail him instead! Why risk putting his personal life out there as fodder for office gossip, especially if you have to go through receptionists or personal secretaries to get to him? He may even share an office with others who can hear his phone conversations. Don't think they won't have a field day with your calls. ("Wow, Catherine sure calls a lot. You two must be serious.") So whenever possible, send him an e-mail, and no one will be the wiser. The less you call him in a public arena, the better!

17. If money is tight and you really cannot afford to pay to be on an online dating service, check out any services that allow you to post a photo with an ad for a free trial period. There are also online dating services that let you post an ad and photo for free so long as you do not write to anyone first but only respond to men who see your ad and photo and write to you first. This is equivalent to a "ladies night" at a bar where women can enjoy free drinks all night. All you have to do is show up: Post your free ad and photo, don't e-mail any men, just sit back and see who e-mails you. As a *Rules* girl, you

should not initiate contact with men first anyway, so this would be a perfect service for you!

18. If you are shy or uncomfortable going to bars and parties, or feel inhibited about your looks (e.g., you are overweight), online dating may be your answer. It takes the edge off the whole meat-market feeling of mingling in person. However, don't make the mistake of posting a photo that doesn't represent your current appearance. Honesty here is definitely still the best policy.

Plan B: Until You Can Do *The Rules* 100 Percent

We sometimes get e-mail and phone queries from women saying that they would love to do *The Rules,* but don't honestly think they can. They find it all too hard and wish there was a more lenient plan we could give them. While in our heart of hearts we believe strictest is best, we understand how they feel and want to accommodate them in some way. We feel it is still better to do *The Rules* a little bit than not at all. Didn't you start on the treadmill thinking you could never do more than a mile and after six months work up to three? Well, that's how we feel about Plan B. It could eventually lead to doing *The Rules* 100 percent, and in the meantime, it's better than no plan at all!

Plan B eliminates any excuses, prevents you from saying, "*The Rules* are so strict, I'll just do whatever I feel like!" That's the worst thing you can do because you will surely end up in pen-pal e-mail relationships that go nowhere, Instant Messaging men until the wee hours of the morning, men who may not even ask you out or who end up saying they are not ready for an exclusive relationship—in short, you'll be wasting your time.

So just because you can't do *The Rules* to the letter, don't use that as license to go wild. Here are some Plan Bs that just might work for you:

The Rules say don't answer men's ads.

Plan B says if you still want to be able to pick and choose potential dates, or if you've already answered a man's ad and you are in a relationship, do all the other *Rules*—don't initiate e-mails, wait 24 hours to respond to men's e-mails, wait for them to ask you out, let them visit you three times before you visit them, and so on.

The Rules say post a photo with your ad.

Plan B says if, for whatever reason, you don't want your photo on the Internet, at least describe yourself in your screen name or in your ad in a physical way. Celebrity lookalike descriptions (i.e., CatherineZeta-JonesLooks29 or GwynethPaltrow-type30) are good for catching the attention of men who typically scan photos since most people are familiar with what these stars look like. You can also use a catchy descriptive screen name to help you stand out, such as TallBlond35 or FoxyBrunette42.

The Rules say wait 24 hours to respond to a man's e-mails in the first few months of a relationship.

Plan B says wait four hours. We understand that 24 hours can seem like forever when you are e-dating a new prospect, so wait at least four hours so you don't seem desperate. Do some work, organize your desk, make a phone call, go to the gym or out to lunch, and when you come back, you can send him a short e-mail. The point is not to e-mail him in nanoseconds or minutes.

The Rules say block yourself so you can't accept Instant Messages.

Plan B says accept Instant Messages from men, but don't initiate them. Then follow all the rest of *The Rules* for IMs— keep the sessions short and make sure you end them first. There is no worse feeling than a guy logging off before you.

The Rules say don't answer men's e-mails on weekends (Friday night through Sunday afternoon) and holidays.

Plan B says answer men's e-mails any time on Sunday as long as you don't do so on Saturday (date) night. This should give extra leeway to those of you who are bored on Sundays. OK, so he won't think you are away for the weekend. But as long as you don't e-mail him on Saturday night, he can still think you are a CUAO.

The Rules say don't discuss all your online dating experiences on the first date as he may just be pumping you for information and not be really interested in dating you.

Plan B says you can say a few harmless things initially. For example, you can tell him (if he asks) a little about one or two of the men you have met online.

The Rules say he must travel to you, and you must wait until he has visited you three times before you visit him.

Plan B says you can visit him after he visits you once, but you cannot make the first visit. How much a man is willing to travel and be inconvenienced to be with you is a barometer for how he feels about you and how he views your relationship. There are other reasons you shouldn't visit a man as often as he visits you. For one thing, a man is less likely to get commitment-phobic or scared if he is visiting you, but he will surely feel that his space is being invaded if you visit him too often.

The Rules say to keep your e-mails light and breezy, on topics such as work and current events, and to ask only casual questions such as "How's your day?"

Plan B says you can say one thing serious about yourself in the first few e-mails, such as you wanted to be a lawyer but dropped out of law school to work for your uncle in the garment center or your parents divorced when you were seven.

The Rules say not to initiate any e-mails in the first three months.

Plan B says it's okay to initiate a short, fun e-mail (such as a forward or joke) occasionally, assuming he is e-mailing you every week.

Final Thoughts from a Psychotherapist

I am an experienced Licensed Master Social Worker–Advanced Clinical Practitioner with a psychotherapy and coaching practice in Houston, Texas. I coach singles internationally to help them meet their relationship goals. And I am an enthusiastic advocate of *The Rules* ever since Ellen Fein and Sherrie Schneider's first publication, *The Rules,* in 1995, through their subsequent books, *The Rules II* and *The Rules for Marriage.* I have my own special *Rules* girl—Sandra—my lovely wife of many years who is a successful self-actualized businesswoman. I credit her for helping to bring about our wedding by following *Rules* principles and for contributing to our happiness together in a *Rules* marriage.

Now I'm thrilled to see that Ellen and Sherrie have brought *The Rules* to dating on the Internet. In my work, I see much anguish and depression among women who are not taking advantage of *The Rules* in their relationships with men—in real life and online. I think Internet dating can be a good way to meet one's match, but only if it is done in the right way. Fortunately, Ellen and Sherrie explain what the right way is in *The Rules for Online Dating*.

I join Ellen and Sherrie in stressing to women that they must:

- beware of becoming too available to a man through e-mail. As is true in inappropriate telephoning of him, e-mail communication can also become a disaster area if a woman frequently e-mails a man and answers every e-mail message he sends to her. All telephone *Rules* apply even more strongly in the e-mail relationship;
- realize that ongoing e-mail communications are no substitute for seeing him in person;
- be careful to check guys out and find out who they are before meeting them and being alone with them, even in a public place.

I am thrilled that Ellen and Sherrie have spoken out with this timely and insightful book. There is nothing like *The Rules* out there in the area of man-woman dating and courting relationship literature. *The Rules for Online Dating* can be of tremendous assistance to any woman who is using e-mail to correspond with men—whether she is initially meeting men in conventional ways but using e-mail to correspond, or using chat rooms and Internet dating services to meet men. Reading *The Rules for Online Dating* before booting up and logging on may save a woman from unnecessary heartache.

Neill Scott, LMSW-ACP

website: http://ve.net*relationships/*

A *RULES* GLOSSARY

A.S.L.: Acronym for Age, Sex, Location. This is a pickup line men use in chat rooms and does not merit a response, as it shows no interest and little effort in meeting you.

Blocking: An online feature that, when activated, prevents anyone from knowing if and when you're online. Blocking yourself on the Internet prevents you from receiving any Instant Messages, though your regular e-mails will come through to your mailbox as usual. Thus, you can be online without anyone knowing it. Blocking is especially useful on weekends, when you may want to be on your computer without letting anyone know you're sitting home on a Saturday night without a date.

Bookmarking: When a man asks you out without any specific date or time ("Let's get together real soon . . ."), do not take it too seriously. Do not ask "When?" or "What did you have in mind?"

Boot Camp: Following *The Rules* extra-strictly after falling off the wagon.

Chat Room: An online forum where people can converse with each other by posting messages in "real time"—that is, the message is transmitted immediately to the room and can be responded to immediately by anyone else who's logged into the room.

Closing the Deal: A term that applies to finding out where a relationship with a man you've been dating for at least a year and a half to two years is going, and not letting it go on indefinitely. Specifically, it means giving a man whom you've been dating for a year and a half an ultimatum to help him propose and ending the relationship if he doesn't.

Creature Unlike Any Other (CUAO): It is the state of mind of a woman (a *Rules* girl) with a sense of confidence and a radiance that permeates her being. She's optimistic, not cynical. She believes in *The Rules* and tries to follow them to the letter. She doesn't go to pieces when a relationship doesn't work out, but brushes away her tears and moves on!

Date Zero: The first date or real-life meeting with an online guy; called "zero" because it's the first time you're meeting a man face-to-face whom you've never seen before, except perhaps in an online photo. In conventional dating, you quite likely have met a man (at a club, through a personal introduction) before he asks you out on a first date, so you know what he looks like in person. DZ is the same as a conventional blind date, except that you've exchanged e-mails beforehand.

Delete/Next!: How to respond to men you are not interested in, such as time-wasters, married men, men who send winks but no words, men who don't send photos, or men who somehow seem suspicious to you. Just hit "delete" on your computer keyboard and move on to the next guy!

Good for Now (GFN): The ever-available, overly accommodating girl who gets dumped when someone more interesting or challenging comes along.

Instant Message (IM): A message that pops up on your online computer screen in real time, and to which you can respond in real time and create a dialog back and forth. With IM, a man knows if and when you're on the computer, and can get you into a conversation in an instant if you respond.

Laughing Out Loud (LOL): Laughing at a guy's joke, just don't overdo it.

Light and Breezy (L&B): How you should be in e-mails and on dates (as opposed to heavy and deep).

Lobster: A potential suitor in online dating; someone who has responded to your personal ad and looks like a live one. A *Rules* girl once referred to checking her e-mail as "off to check the lobster traps" and the expression stuck.

Long-Distance Relationship (LDR): Let him visit you!

Love Only Those Who Love You: As a result of doing *The Rules,* you are no longer interested in men who are not interested in you, who ignore you, cheat on you, or any man who can live without you. You love being loved. You have no desire to chase someone who hasn't noticed you and sought you out. Sound obvious? You'd be surprised at how many women go after men who don't want them.

Moon Pie: A man who stares and stares but never approaches. He could be shy or psychotic or just not that interested. In the online world, this would be a man who e-mails you but never asks you out.

Next!: What a *Rules* girl says when she has to move on, break up. Dump-o-rama!

Nothing: What a *Rules* girl tells another about a non-relationship: It's just pure fantasy on a woman's part. Some women think a guy is interested in them because of bookmarking or flimsy e-mails and calls—all nothing if there haven't been any dates! He may even be her dentist or ENT (Ear, Nose, and Throat) doctor, and he seems very caring about her mouth or her nose, he may even call her in between appointments after her root canal or new antibiotic nose spray is administered, but she never sees him outside of her appointments!

Online Dating Service: Websites—such as love@aol.com, match.com, matchmaker.com, jdate.com, personals.yahoo.com, to name only a few—in which men and women post ads and photos of themselves in order to meet new people. Usually, you can list your ad and photo for free, but to respond to ads, you must subscribe to the website and pay a monthly fee.

Poof!: A disappearing act by a man who comes on hot and heavy in his first e-mail or two and then you never hear from him again.

Pretzel Brain Twist (PBT): Unnecessary analysis and angst that get women all worked up and do nothing to change the situation, usually accompanied by waiting by the phone, eating doughnuts, and endless conversations with frustrated girlfriends who have to listen to all their crazy talk.

Professional Single: Confirmed bachelor, always online or at singles events, but nothing ever happens. (See **Nothing**; **Bookmark**; **Moon Pie**.)

Real Life (RL): As opposed to online only.

***Rules* Girl (RG):** Girl who sets boundaries and in the first three months of dating doesn't let it all hang out, but has grace and dignity and lets her feelings out one by one in time. She also believes in old-fashioned "playing hard to get"!

Time-Waster: An online guy who appears to be normal but asks a million questions, usually philosophical ones like, "What did you learn from your last relationship?" or "Where do you see yourself in five years?" but cannot ask you for your phone number. Or he gets your number, but always has an e-mail excuse as to why he can't call or see you.

Wink: An impersonal, stock message (i.e., a wink of the eye) you can send in an e-mail by the push of a key. On a dating website, men sometimes send winks in response to a woman's ad and photo—an easy and casual response since it requires no writing at all. We tell women not to answer men who send winks, as these men have made no effort to personalize their response to your ad— they've written nothing, not even a simple line or two, to show they've read your ad. They may have clicked on dozens (or hundreds) of women's ads, including yours, and sent winks out to you and them, without singling your ad out in any special way.

WUMTHS: Waiting Until Marriage to Have Sex. There are also many women who are WAWAWTHS (waiting and waiting and waiting . . .) LOL!

For more information about *The Rules,* including

- *The Rules News* Newsletter
- Website (www.therulesbook.com)
- Private consultations with the authors
- *Rules* seminars
- *Rules* audiotapes and videotapes
- *Rules* merchandise including *Rules* Ankle Bracelets (oval plate with CUAO inscribed on it, in silver and gold), and more,

please contact:

> *The Rules*
> FDR Station
> P.O. Box 6047
> New York, NY 10150
> (212) 388-7910 (phone), (973) 422-0048 (fax)